The hands-on guide to post

for school sixth forms, training providers, and further education colleges in 2008/09

D0489444

Nick Linford
Director of Planning and Performance
Lewisham College
London, UK

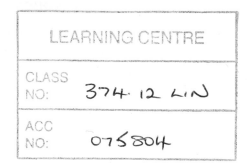

This book is as balanced, practical and accurate as I could make it.
Ideas for improvements are always welcome via email to:
nick.linford@fundingguide.co.uk

For further information and updates visit www.fundinggu

The hands-on guide to post-16 funding
First published September 2008
Second impression 2009

Text © 2008 Nick Linford

Edexcel Limited
190 High Holborn
London WC1V 7BH, UK

Book orders can be placed by telephone or via the website.
To order via the website, please go to: www.edexcel.org.uk/fundingguide

ISBN 978-1-8469-0390-8

Linford, N (Nick)
The hands-on guide to post-16 funding
Illustrations by Nick Linford, London, UK
Typesetting and page layout by The Publishing Centre, Oxford, UK
Printed in Great Britain by Henry Ling Ltd., at the Dorset Press, Dorchester, Dorset

We are grateful to the following for their permission to reproduce copyright material:
Page 11: extract from *Realising the Potential, A review of the future role of further education colleges*, Sir Andrew Foster (November 2005).
Page 11: extract from *Leitch Review of Skills* (December 2006).
Page 13: extract from *2007 Comprehensive Spending Review*, HM Treasury (October 2007).
Page 17: extract from *Our Statement of Priorities – Better Skills, Better Jobs, Better Lives*, LSC (November 2007). Page 21: extract from *The 16–18, Adult Learner- and Employer-responsive Funding Models – update*, LSC (June 2008)
Page 51: extract from *LSC Grant Letter 2006/07*, October 2005
Page 11: diagram from *2007 Comprehensive Spending Review*, HM Treasury (October 2007).
Page 12: diagram from *2007 Comprehensive Spending Review and LSC Grant Letter 2008–09*, DIUS (November 2007).
Page 12: diagram from 2007 *Comprehensive Spending Review and LSC Grant Letter 2008–09*, DIUS (November 2007).
Page 14: diagram and figures from *LSC Grant Letter 2008–09*.
Page 14: diagram and figures from *LSC Annual Accounts*.
Page 15: diagram from *LSC Funding Rates – Changes for 2007/08*, LSC (January 2007)
Page 16: diagram and figures from *LSC Grant Letter 2008/09*, DIUS (November 2007)
Page 16: table and figures from *LSC Grant Letter 2008/09*, DIUS (November 2007)
Page 18: graph from *Our Statement of Priorities – Better Skills, Better Jobs, Better Lives*, LSC (November 2007)
Page 18: figures from *LSC Grant Letter 2008–09*, DIUS (November 2007)
Page 19: graph from *Our Statement of Priorities – Better Skills, Better Jobs, Better Lives*, LSC (November 2007)
Page 23: figures from *The Funding Gap*, KPMG (January 2008)
Page 23: diagram from *The 16–18, Adult Learner- and Employer-responsive Funding Models*, LSC (June 2008)
Page 25: diagram from *Our Statement of Priorities – Better Skills, Better Jobs, Better Lives*, LSC (November 2007)
Page 82: diagram from *The Diploma: an overview of the qualification*, QCA, Version 3, 2008
Page 84: diagram from *The Diploma: an overview of the qualification*, QCA, Version 3, 2008
Page 86: diagram from *The Diploma: an overview of the qualification*, QCA, Version 3, 2008

Every effort has been made to trace the copyright holders and we apologise in advance for any unintentional omissions. We would be pleased to insert the appropriate acknowledgment in any subsequent edition of this publication.

Content overview

Detailed Contents

Glossary of abbreviations

AFI: Assumed Fee Income

ALN: Additional Learning Needs

ALS: Additional Learning Support

ALSN: Additional Learning and Support Needs

ASL: Adult Safeguarded Learning

ASN: Additional Social Needs

CSR: Comprehensive Spending Review

DCSF: Department for Children, Schools and Families

DIUS: Department for Innovation, Universities and Skills

E2E: Entry to Employment

EFL: English as a Foreign Language

EfW: ESOL for Work

ESOL: English for Speakers of Other Languages

FE: further education

FEFC: Further Education and Funding Council

FfE: Framework for Excellence

FLT: Foundation Learning Tier

FTE: full-time equivalent

glh: guided learning hour

HE: higher education

HEFCE: Higher Education and Funding Council for England

HEI: Higher Education Institution

IELTS: International English Language Testing System

ILR: Individualised Learner Record

LAD: Learning Aim Database

LLDD: Learners with Learning Difficulties and/or Disabilities

LSC: Learning and Skills Council

LSF: Learner Support Funding

MLP: Minimum Levels of Performance

NBR: National Base Rate

NDAQ: National Database of Accredited Qualifications

NDPB: Non-Departmental Public Bodies

NEET: Not in Education, Employment or Training

NFR: National funding rate

NQF: National Qualifications Framework

NVQ: National Vocational Qualification

OLASS: Offender Learning And Skills Service

OLDC: Online Data Collection Portal

PaMS: Planning and Modelling System

PF: provider factor

PSA: Public Service Agreement

QAA: Quality Assurance Agency

QCA: Qualification and Curriculum Authority

QCF: Qualification and Credit Framework

SfBN: Skills for Business Network

SfJ: Skills for Jobs

SLN: Standard Learner Number

SSoA: Summary Statement of Activity

TtG: Train to Gain

UKVQRP: UK Vocational Qualification Reform Programme

WBL: Work-based learning

Author's introduction

The hands-on guide to post-16 funding is for anyone with an interest in Learning and Skills Council (LSC) 16–18, adult learner-responsive or employer-responsive funding. As such, it covers the new 2008/09 national funding formula and demand-led models for school sixth form, further education (16–18 and adult), Apprenticeship, Entry to Employment and Train to Gain provision. It is designed to be used as a reference tool rather than read from cover to cover. However, and most importantly, *this guide is not the authoritative source of LSC information on funding*, as that is of course published by the LSC. This guide is simply a complementary tool that I hope helps to summarise the information and implications of LSC funding rates, eligibility and methodology. Funding is a complex topic and this guide is unable to cover all the finer details, and elements may quickly become out of date (the LSC may change rates and rules during the year).

I am fortunate enough to work with the LSC as a member of its technical funding advisory group, which was established in 2005 to consider the implications of reforming the funding formula, methodology and rates. This gives me an insight into the work of the LSC funding policy team, who I believe do a sterling job balancing competing demands to increase simplicity while maintaining fairness (*see page 29*). However, the true privilege is working for Lewisham College, a large and successful college that makes a significant difference to the lives of many in South East London. As a Director at the College, I plan provision and report on performance, as well as meeting regularly with the LSC. I have therefore written this book as a provider for providers, and I want it to be useful to those in the sector, particularly those planning and delivering provision, who want to understand where the funding comes from, what it funds and how much it will generate for some of the most popular qualifications. This information should not only be interesting, but also practical, in that it can be used in the curriculum planning and performance cycle to help achieve a variety of targets and performance measures.

The guide is split into sections; within each section a topic is covered across two pages. This serves two purposes. Firstly, it should make it easier for you to find information (without the need for an index). Secondly, two pages per topic means I have had a volume constraint, which, given the complexity of the topic, is probably welcome.

Finally, I would like to take this opportunity to acknowledge and thank a number of people: Siân Owen at Edexcel for all her hard work and being the driving force behind this book; Bob Osborne at Edexcel for believing in the idea and backing it financially; Julian Gravatt, Alex Cook, John Callaghan, Stewart Segal and Mark Dunkerley for being expert readers; Dame Ruth Silver and Stephen Lawes at Lewisham College for supporting me throughout, and last but by no-means least, thanks are due to Sandra and Denis Linford and Sarah, my beautiful partner, for keeping me sane and happy.

Comments from across the sector

I am delighted to be able to sponsor and publish this book on funding and I am confident it will prove an invaluable resource for you, our centres. We all know that an effective understanding of funding can have huge impact in determining the successful running of a college and in turn the educational performance of the learners within it.

We are committed to supporting our centres, constantly innovating to provide a better service, and this book, alongside the LSC guidance, helps you understand funding for the broad range of post-16 provision on offer to your learners.

Jerry Jarvis, Managing Director, Edexcel

Lewisham College is proud to be behind the publication of this book which will help our sector navigate their way through the emerging complexity at this time of change. As a college we recognise the importance of being both clear in purpose and outstanding in results. This book is a resource which enables Lewisham College to not only deliver the outstanding successes that we are known for, but also to help us to do it with intelligence and sensitivity. We are glad to have it.

Dame Ruth Silver, Principal, Lewisham College and Chair of the Learning and Skills Improvement Service (LSIS)

Colleges will find 2008 a particularly challenging year. Tighter budgets, ambitious targets, pressure of numbers, new qualifications and systems re-shaping will all play a part in the interesting times ahead. Alongside all this, colleges will be grappling with the new funding formula and this book should prove an invaluable guide. A must-have for anyone concerned with funding in the further education system.

Julian Gravatt, Director of Funding and Development, Association of Colleges (AoC)

The ALP are delighted that demand-led funding has been agreed as the right way forward in advancing the Government's skills strategy. The expansion of apprenticeships and the additional Train to Gain flexibilities are also very positive steps and a significant opportunity for work-based learning providers and the employers they work with. This guide will be welcomed by our members: the practical approach to funding will help build their knowledge and understanding in order to respond to the changing funding system with confidence.

**Graham Hoyle, Chief Executive of the
Association of Learning Providers (ALP)**

The new LSC plan-led funding system brings with it significant changes to the way school sixth forms are funded. Amongst the key changes are a new funding formula using individual school success rates rather than the national average, a funding cap set at the level equivalent to 4.25 AS/A-levels per student, a change in the way Additional Learning Support funding is distributed and the use of retrospective data. This book, which explains the sixth form funding system in simple and straightforward terms, will be a useful tool for anyone getting to grips with the complex world of post-16 funding.

**Malcolm Trobe, National Council Member (LSC), former President of the
Association of School and College Leaders (ASCL), former Headteacher,
Malmesbury School and now Policy Director ASCL**

Whilst this book is clearly not associated with, endorsed by, or written by the LSC, it may well prove to be valuable for those readers wanting to know where the 08/09 funding system came from, how the principles work (in some detail) and Nick's view of where it is going. Nick is a well-respected member of the FE sector who has an excellent understanding of the funding system and how it works in practice.

**Alex Cook, Senior Funding Policy Implementation Manager,
Learning and Skills Council (LSC)**

The context

The Government's current investment strategy in post-16 education and training is to a great extent in direct response to an increasingly global and competitive economy. Their latest estimates are that 'by 2017, China and India will have nearly doubled their share of world income and are likely to be bigger than the UK, French and German economies combined'.

Asian economies' share of world GDP in 1950 and 2020
Source: 2007 *Comprehensive Spending Review,* HM Treasury (October 2007)

1950 — 18.5%

2020 projected — 30.3%

Education and training are considered a part of the solution to this economic competition, and in 2004 the Government commissioned Sir Andrew Foster to review the future role of colleges. Foster concluded that colleges 'should adopt as their primary purpose, improving employability and supplying economically valuable skills'.

> The UK has a prosperous history but our future depends on our skills. The world is a competitive market and the marketplace is crowded with nations seeking to succeed. Newer entrants to the market – China for example – can call on fantastic numbers of increasingly skilful people. The world being as it is, the UK cannot assume that its future will be like its past: it truly may not be.
>
> Source: *Realising the Potential, A review of the future role of further education colleges,* Sir Andrew Foster (November 2005)

Also in 2004, the Treasury commissioned Lord Sandy Leitch to undertake an independent review of the UK's long-term skills needs and concluded that 'the UK's skills base remains mediocre by international standards'. Leitch reinforced Foster's findings that there is a strong and direct link between a nation's skill level and its economic success:

> To achieve world class prosperity and fairness in the new global economy, the UK must achieve world class skills. Without world class skills, UK businesses will find it increasingly difficult to compete and innovate. The employment opportunities of the lowest skilled will continue to decline, risking a lost generation, cut off permanently from labour market opportunity. The Review has concluded that, where skills were once a key driver of prosperity and fairness, they are now *the* key driver. Achieving world class skills is the key to achieving economic success and social justice in the new global economy.
>
> Source: *Leitch Review of Skills,* HM Treasury (December 2006)

The *Leitch Review of Skills* soon led to the Government publishing *World Class Skills: Implementing the Leitch Review of Skills in England*, DIUS (July 2007). Therefore, many of the current funding-related priorities and targets described within the following pages (particularly for adults) can be traced back to the recommendations made in the Leitch review.

Government funding

In June 2007 the Department for Education and Skills (DfES) was replaced by two new departments: the Department for Children, Schools and Families (DCSF) aims to 'make England the best place in the world for children and young people to grow up' and oversees education and funding for those up to the age of 18; the Department for Innovation, Universities and Skills (DIUS) aims to 'apply both knowledge and skills to create an innovative and competitive economy' and oversees education and funding for those beyond the age of 18. The DCSF and DIUS receive funding from the Treasury, and pass some of this on to the Learning and Skills Council (LSC) to fund providers that deliver education and training.

The 2008–09 projected flow of government funding

Source: 2007 *Comprehensive Spending Review,* HM Treasury (October 2007) and *LSC Grant Letter 2008–09,* DIUS (November 2007)

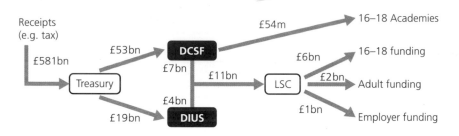

The year 2008/09 is the first year of the Government's 2007–2010 Comprehensive Spending Review (CSR). This means that funding has been projected over the next three years, up to and including 2010/11. The three-year projection, when combined with spending in 2007/08, means that overall funding for participation will continue to rise above inflation.

LSC budget for participation, including specialist provision

Source: 2007 *Comprehensive Spending Review,* HM Treasury (October 2007) and *LSC Grant Letter 2008–09,* DIUS (November 2007)

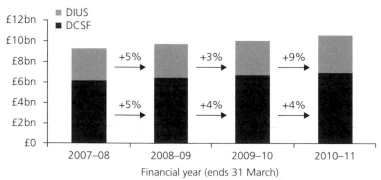

However, this real-terms growth in funding comes with important strings attached, known as Public Service Agreements (PSA) and national targets. There are 30 PSAs that cover all government departments, and will to a great extent dictate what is, and what is not, an LSC funding priority from 2008/09 until 2010.

Three of the 30 PSAs relate to post-16 education and training, and each PSA contains a number of measurable national targets.

DCSF is the lead department responsible for:

1. Raising the educational achievement of all young people by:

   increasing the proportion of young people achieving Level 2 at age 19 from 71% in 2005/06 to 82% in 2010/11;

   increasing the proportion of young people achieving Level 3 at age 19 from 47% in 2005/06 to 54% in 2010/11.

2. Increasing the number of young people on the path to success by:

   reducing from 10% in 2004 the number of 16–18-year-olds not in education, employment or training (NEET) by two percentage points.

DIUS is the lead department responsible for:

3. Improving the skills of the population by:

   ensuring 597,000 adults achieve their first Level 1, or above, literacy (or ESOL) qualification, and 390,000 achieve a first Entry Level 3, or above, numeracy qualification from 2008/09 to 2010/11;

   increasing the proportion of working age adults qualified to at least full Level 2 from 70% in 2006 to 79% by 2011;

   increasing the proportion of working age adults qualified to at least full Level 3 from 49% in 2006 to 56% by 2011;

   ensuring 130,000 apprentices complete the full Apprenticeship Framework in 2010/11 (a rise from 98,000 in 2005/06);

   increasing the proportion of working age adults qualified to Level 4 and above from 30% in 2006 to 34% in 2011 and to 36% in 2014;

   increasing participation in higher education, of those aged 18–30, from 43% in 2005/06 towards 50% by 2010 [progression from FE important].

As described within the following pages, funding is heavily prioritised for qualifications that can deliver these PSA national targets. Conversely, funding will continue to reduce for provision that does not.

Learning and Skills Council

The Learning and Skills Council (LSC) is the largest Non-Departmental Public Body (NDPB), which, in 2001, took over the roles of the former Further Education Funding Council and Training and Enterprise Councils. The LSC is responsible for planning and funding education and training in England for nearly everyone over the age of 15, other than those in universities. For the 2008–09 period, the LSC has been allocated £11.4 billion by the Government to spend as follows:

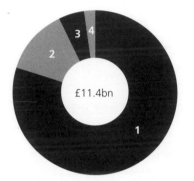

LSC Budget 2008–09

Source: *LSC Grant Letter 2008–09*, DIUS (November 2007)

1. learning participation (80%)
2. learner support and development (13%)
3. capital grants (5%)
4. LSC administration (2%)

The LSC has a head office in Coventry, but plans and funds delivery from nine regional offices and through partnership teams that cover broadly the same areas as the approximately 150 local authorities in England.

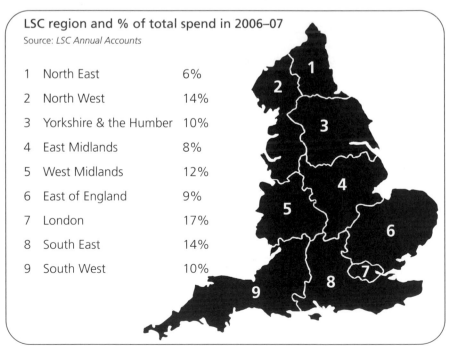

LSC region and % of total spend in 2006–07

Source: *LSC Annual Accounts*

1	North East	6%
2	North West	14%
3	Yorkshire & the Humber	10%
4	East Midlands	8%
5	West Midlands	12%
6	East of England	9%
7	London	17%
8	South East	14%
9	South West	10%

In addition to planning and funding delivery, the LSC is responsible for devising and maintaining the funding methodology, formula and relative qualification rates for all the funding models in 2008/09. Therefore, if you are seeking the definitive funding guidance, the following key 2008/09 documents are published and updated by the LSC and can be found on their website:

1. *Funding Rates for 2008/09*, LSC (may be merged with Funding Formula document)
2. *Funding Principles, Rules and Regulations*, LSC
3. *Funding Compliance Advice and Audit Guidance 2008/09*, LSC
4. *Funding Formula for 2008/09*, LSC
5. *Learner Eligibility Guidance*, LSC
6. *Funding Claims and Audit Returns*
7. *Addendum to Funding Guidance* (if required during 2008/09)

Therefore, while this practical guide brings to life the funding formula and methodology, the LSC documents should be referred to as the definitive guidance. This is particularly true of the addendum document, as in previous years the funding guidance has been updated during the year.

The funding formula for 2008/09 represents the second new formula introduced by the LSC. The first was in 2002/03, when the qualification currency of units was replaced by a cash base rate. In 2008/09 the cash base rate is to be replaced by a Standard Learner Number (SLN). Arguably, this is a return to a unit-based currency, in which units are called SLNs (*see page 32*).

Note

Although the new methodology will remain for the foreseeable future, every year the LSC changes some qualification rates. In the example below, the LSC used actual delivery durations in 2005/06 as evidence to justify a rate reduction for a popular qualification type in 2008/09.

18-unit Level 3 GNVQ successor (e.g. BTEC National Diploma)

Source: *LSC Funding Rates – Changes for 2007/08*, LSC (January 2007)

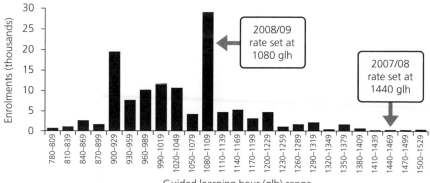

16–18 funding

The new Department for Children, Schools and Families (DCSF) is responsible for allocating funding to the LSC for learners up to the age of 18. This funding sits within the new 16–18 funding model, and in 2008/09 the DCSF allocation will be in excess of £6bn.

Planned 16–18 funding: England 2008/09

Source: *LSC Grant Letter 2008/09*, DIUS (November 2007) (excluding specialist provision)

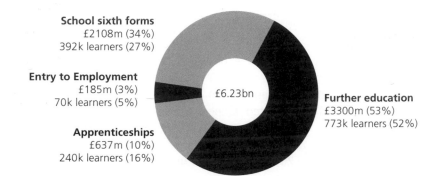

School sixth forms
£2108m (34%)
392k learners (27%)

Entry to Employment
£185m (3%)
70k learners (5%)

£6.23bn

Further education
£3300m (53%)
773k learners (52%)

Apprenticeships
£637m (10%)
240k learners (16%)

Increasing 16–18-year-old participation is a key priority, paid for by a 9% funding rise by 2010/11 (including inflation). However, this masks important projected shifts in learner numbers within the new 16–18 funding model.

Projected 16–18-year-old learners in England

Source: *LSC Grant Letter 2008/09*, DIUS (November 2007) (excluding specialist provision)

16–18 Funding model	Learners in 07/08	Shift to 08/09	Shift to 10/11	General shift
Further Education	773,000	0%	0%	▬
of which full-time	655,000	+1%	+2%	↑
of which part-time	117,000	–3%	–9%	⬇
Apprenticeships	238,000	+1%	+18%	⬆
Entry to Employment	70,000	0%	0%	▬
School sixth forms	391,000	0%	0%	▬
of which maintained	382,000	–2%	–5%	↓
of which academies (directly DCSF funded)	9000	+78%	+211%	⬆
Total 16–18 learners	1,472,000	0%	3%	↑

> Even though the 16–18 age group peaks in 2008/09 and then declines by 65,000 by 2010/11, we plan to increase the total number of learners in the 16–18 group funded by the LSC by 59,000 – from 1,457,000 in 2006/07 to 1,516,000 in 2010/11.
>
> Source: *Our Statement of Priorities – Better Skills, Better Jobs, Better Lives*, LSC (November 2007)

Further education

The projected demand from 16–18-year-old learners within colleges will remain at approximately 773,000 for the next three years. However, full-time learners will increase by just over 10,000 and part-time learners will decrease by a similar number. This is important, as it not only means that in the face of a demographic downturn an increase in full-time learners is still projected for colleges, but also that the average funding per 16–18-year-old learner in further education must rise above inflation. In the new funding model this is referred to as a rise in the Standard Learner Number (SLN) per learner ratio *(see page 50)*.

Apprenticeships

Although 16–18 Apprenticeships are planned and budgeted for by the DCSF and from the 16–18 funding model, because apprentices are by definition employed learners, the providers are paid in-year, according to rates and rules within DIUS's employer-responsive funding model. The 16–18 Apprenticeship growth projection for 2008/09 is a modest 2000 learners (1%), but this will rise to a not insignificant additional 43,000 (18%) learners by 2010/11. Learner places will of course require employer commitment, which will be all the more important from 2012, when the Government 'introduces an entitlement to an Apprenticeship place for every young person aged 16–18 who attains the entry qualifications required by the sector'. Programme-led Apprenticeships can engage learners prior to employment.

Entry to Employment (E2E)

E2E is a programme designed for hard-to-reach learners who are, or are in danger of being, not in education, employment or training (NEET). The projection is that the number of learners funded as E2E will remain constant, but over time E2E will be assimilated into other programmes below Level 2 within Progression Pathways as part of the new Foundation Learning Tier (FLT).

School sixth forms

Perhaps the biggest funding methodology change in 2008/09 is for maintained school sixth forms, who join the further education sector within the new national funding formula. Interestingly, it is projected that, unlike colleges, their full-time learners will fall by 18,000 by 2010/11. This is likely to be as a result of a demographic downturn and a number of maintained schools becoming academies. The number of school sixth form academies is projected to expand rapidly. Their funding is also calculated in line with the new LSC national funding formula, but unlike maintained school sixth forms they are paid directly by the DCSF.

Adult and employer funding

The Department for Innovation, Universities and Skills (DIUS) is keen to distinguish funding for adult (19+) part-time training within the workplace from funding for full-time and part-time adults studying on college premises. Therefore, from 2008/09 two new, demand-led funding models have been created: the employer-responsive funding model and the adult learner-responsive funding model. Importantly, a shift is taking place from the college-based learner-responsive funding model to the workplace-based employer-responsive funding model:

Projected learners in adult learner-responsive funding models

Source: *Our Statement of Priorities – Better Skills, Better Jobs, Better Lives*, LSC (November 2007)

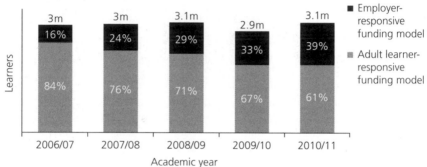

The shift from adult-learner to employer provision is designed to make the system responsive to employers, and to achieve the Government's adult Public Service Agreement (PSA) targets in 2010/11:

• increasing the number of adults with literacy and numeracy skills;
• increasing the number of adults achieving a first full Level 2;
• increasing the number of adults achieving a first full Level 3;
• increasing the number of adults achieving an Apprenticeship.

The employer-responsive funding model consists of Apprenticeships and Train to Gain provision, nearly all of which contribute to one or more of these targets. In contrast, the adult learner-responsive funding model funds a significant volume of provision that does not contribute to these PSA targets. This 'non-priority' learning has been categorised in 2008/09 as 'developmental learning' and here funding continues to be cut significantly:

Developmental learning in adult learner-responsive funding model

Source: *LSC Grant Letter 2008–09* , DIUS (November 2007)

2008/09	£386m	No figures for previous year
2009/10	£191m	£195m (50%) reduction
2010/11	£106m	£85m (45%) reduction

The LSC grant letter outlines in great detail how the overall adult demand-led formula funding is increasing by 19%, from £2.6bn in 2007/08 to just over £3bn in 2010/11. However, perhaps more useful in terms of understanding this projected expansion of funding is the graph on page 26 of the *LSC Statement of Priorities 2008/09 to 2010/11*. This graph is shown below (it excludes non-formula funded Adult Safeguarded Learning and specialist learning for learners with learning difficulties and/or disabilities).

Projected expansion of demand-led funding

Source: *Our Statement of Priorities – Better Skills, Better Jobs, Better Lives*, LSC (November 2007)

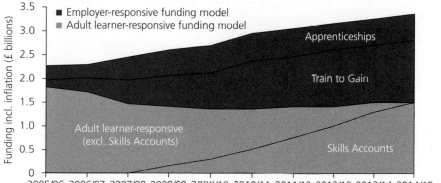

This graph demonstrates the following:
* a nine-year trend from 2005/06 to 2014/15;
* a switch from learner to employer funding and all to be demand-led;
* a steady and significant increase in Train to Gain funding following the national roll-out in 2006/07;
* the introduction of Skills Accounts, which will fund all adult learner-responsive provision by 2014/15;
* by 2014/15 funding will be split 50:50 between learner and employer.

It is clear from the graph that the projected expansion of demand-led funding supports the recommendations of the *Leitch Review of Skills* to 'route all vocational skills public funding in England, apart from community learning, through Train to Gain and Skills Accounts by 2010'. The two exceptions to this, i.e. where activity does not closely follow the Leitch recommendations, are the continued support of the Apprenticeships and the four-year delay in the shift to this model.

The LSC has overseen the creation of 16–18, adult learner- and employer-responsive funding models for 2008/09, and the creation of two new government departments reinforces the age divide at 19. The next chapter takes a closer look at the three funding models and outlines some of their key differences (particularly between the adult learner and employer models).

The models

In November 2007 the LSC published a document that heralded the end of the funding stream. From 2008/09, a variety of post-16 funding streams have been replaced by three new funding models:

> The new funding arrangements for 2008/09 will include separate funding models for 16–18 provision, adult learner-responsive provision and employer-responsive provision as well as a new national funding formula.
>
> The 16–18 model will feature strategic commissioning without reconciliation for all grant-funded providers. Apprenticeships for 16–18-year-olds will be planned and budgeted through this model, but funding will be calculated using the employer-responsive funding model for 2008/09.
>
> The 19+ adult learner-responsive funding model will feature strategic commissioning with mid-year and year-end reconciliation.
>
> The employer-responsive funding model will encompass Train to Gain (Skills for Life, full Levels 2, 3 and above, and employer-based national vocational qualifications (NVQs) currently funded through the further education (FE) funding system) and Apprenticeships. Funding earned by providers will be based on actual delivery, with monthly payment in arrears.
>
> Source: *The 16–18, Adult Learner- and Employer-responsive Funding Models* – update, LSC (June 2008)

The move from five funding streams to three funding models

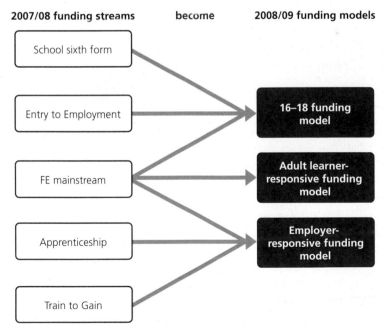

Allocations for all three funding models apply the same national funding formula, but with different contracts, targets, rates, eligibility, monitoring and payment methods. This section takes a closer look at each of the new funding models.

21

16–18 funding model

The 16–18 model replaces three funding streams. This will impact on school sixth forms, colleges and independent training providers.

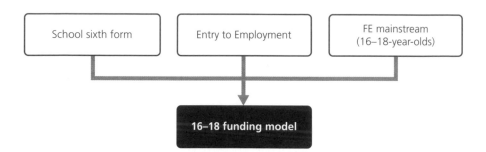

Definition of a learner within the 16–18 funding model:

- 'Aged 16, 17 or 18 on 31 August in the teaching year when the learner begins a programme of study. This wider definition ensures that the funding eligibility of a 16–18-year-old learner does not change during an individual's programme if the learner becomes 19 years old.'

This is a wider definition than that used by the Government for monitoring purposes as it may include some 19-year-olds. It is also different from the definition of 16–18-year-old Apprenticeships in the employer model, which is based on the age of the learner at the start of the programme.

The 16–18 funding model has the following attributes:

- Funding allocations within the 16–18 model are based on the 'plan-led' principle. This means that the LSC allocates funds based on planned delivery and then the allocation is paid, regardless of over- or under-delivery against the plan. Therefore, funding in the 16–18 model is relatively stable during the year, as it is paid monthly to an agreed profile, without fear of 'reconciliation'. However, the LSC may alter the allocation in the plan for the following year to take account of over- or under-performance. Independent providers, such as those delivering Entry to Employment, will also not be subject to reconciliation, but monitoring arrangements may lead to in-year adjustments to their profile and their maximum contract value.
- A new national funding formula is used, as described in the next chapter. Within this formula there are some differences in terms of the way it is applied. For example, school sixth forms only use listed Standard Learner Number values whilst Entry to Employment funding is based on the number of weeks a learner is on-programme.

- Although the new national funding formula is used for both school sixth forms and colleges, the national funding rates are not the same. In 2008/09 school sixth forms will have a national funding rate of £2945, while colleges will be funded at £2860. This represents a 3% 'funding gap', which means school sixth forms will receive 3% more funding for identical provision. In fact, owing to differences in the way non-formula-based activities are funded, the latest research puts the full extent of the gap at above 5%. As the graph below shows, this gap has narrowed sharply in the last few years.

The school sixth form and college 'funding gap'
Source: *The Funding Gap*, KPMG (January 2008)

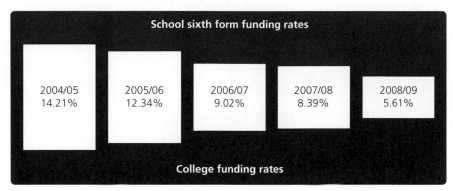

- 16–18-year-olds are fully funded as they are automatically eligible for fee-remission funding.
- 16–18-year-old Apprenticeships are planned and budgeted for by the DCSF and from within the 16–18 funding model. However, their funding will be paid via the employer-responsive model (*see page 26*).
- Learners of this age are a particularly high priority, especially as the Government moves towards 100 per cent participation in some form of training. Much of this growth will come from Apprenticeships.

16–18 model provider allocations are based on:
Source: *The 16–18, Adult Learner- and Employer-responsive Funding Models*, LSC (June 2008)

Adult learner-responsive funding model

Adult learners, with the exception of those enrolled on NVQs delivered within the workplace, will be funded from the new adult learner-responsive funding model.

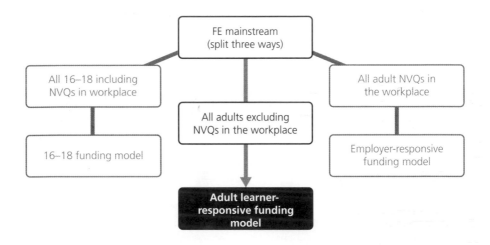

The funding system for this model excludes Adult Safeguarded Learning (ASL) and is very similar to that developed for 16–18 provision. However, there are some important differences for adult learner-responsive funding:

- Adult learners have a national funding rate of £2775. This rate is 3% lower than for 16–18-year-olds in college and 6% cent lower than for school sixth forms, which is explained in more detail on page 34.
- Adults have two funding rates per Standard Learner Number, the fully funded rate and the co-funded rate. The co-funded rate is used when adults are ineligible for fee remission. This means the fee element is deducted from the funding by way of a co-funded rate. In 2008/09 the fee element is 42.5% of the unweighted funding, which is described in detail in the fees section on page 46.
- The adult model includes provision above Level 1, which neither contributes to, nor has the potential to contribute to, Government targets. This 'developmental learning' is being cut year on year.
- The aim, as outlined in the LSC document *Our Statement of Priorities – Better Skills, Better Jobs, Better Lives*, LSC (November 2007), is that all adult-responsive funding will be via Skills Accounts (currently being piloted). This includes a timetable as part of the UK Vocational Qualification Reform Programme (UKVQRP) and the introduction of the Qualification and Credit Framework (QCF) to fund only those qualifications that are classed as a high priority.

Projected shift in adult learner-responsive model funding

Source: *Our Statement of Priorities – Better Skills, Better Jobs, Better Lives*, LSC (November 2007)

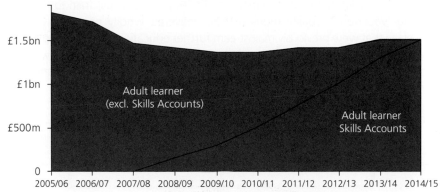

Academic year (figures are indicative)

- The allocation is paid to providers using a monthly profile (similar to 16–18 provision), but there is the introduction of a mid-year and final reconciliation payment. This means that there will be additional payments for over-performance and claw-back for under-performance. The amount of funding available for redistribution will depend on the amount recovered. It is likely that any growth payments for over-performance will be limited to defined LSC priorities and capped at a maximum value, such as 5% of the provider's priority adult allocation once the tolerance of 5% has been exceeded. Further details will be published by the LSC in 2008/09.

- As described above, this approach to reconciliation of actual delivery to planned delivery puts additional pressure on accurate data collection and applying the funding guidance accurately. This linking of payment directly to delivery volumes (funding earned) means that data audits will be required to validate returns made to the LSC. The LSC are currently piloting an extension to the risk-based approach to audit. This means that providers are risk assessed, and the LSC will audit those that are identified as higher risk more frequently. Low- risk providers will receive less frequent visits.

- Adult learner-responsive funding claims are made with 16–18 funding claims. These adult learner-responsive (LR) claims are in the form of an Individualised Learner Record (ILR). The LR ILR is uploaded to the LSC Online Data Collection Portal (OLDC) three times during the year and a minimum of twice after the year has finished (capturing achievement and destination data). Many of the ILR data fields and requirements have changed for 2008/09, so it is important that providers take account of these changes in their learner-records systems and on their enrolment forms. The Information Authority (IA) has taken on responsibility for the ILR, and they follow a timetable in which requests for changes and/or additions to the ILR can be made for future years. The Information Authority website (www.theia.org.uk) contains the ILR specification and related annexes.

Employer-responsive funding model

The employer-responsive funding model funds Apprenticeships, Train to Gain and National Vocational Qualifications (NVQs) delivered wholly or partially in the workplace that were previously mainstream further education (FE). The scope of the employer-responsive funding model is shown in the diagram below, which demonstrates that in broad terms it funds Apprenticeships for all ages and adult learners enrolled on Train to Gain.

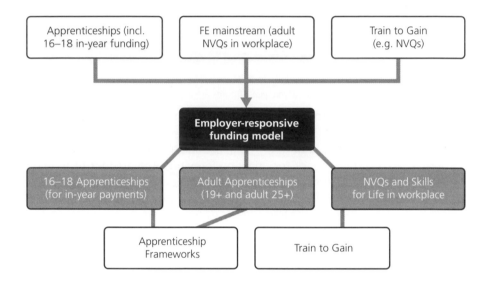

The Apprenticeship Framework is made up of components such as an NVQ, technical certificate and key skills qualifications, plus a funding element called an Apprenticeship element. Apprenticeships for 16–18 and 19+ are funded using the employer-responsive system for calculating funding and making payments. Further information can be found on page 94.

Train to Gain funding is primarily used for NVQs and Skills for Life qualifications that are delivered to adults within the workplace, for which the funding and volume of providers continues to increase (see page 96).

Note

The Apprenticeship and Train to Gain funding return will continue to be made together on a monthly basis. However, the deadline has been shortened by six days, from the tenth to the fourth working day of the month.

The employer-responsive funding model uses the same national funding formula as the 16–18 and adult learner-responsive models, but there are a number of significant differences. These are listed on the table opposite.

Employer-responsive funding model	16–18 and adult learner-responsive funding models
Monthly instalments in which payments are calculated for each enrolment from actual delivery.	Payments monthly on an agreed profile not actual delivery (with some reconciliation for adults).
Payments based on actual weightings within the provider factor for each enrolment.	Payments based on final allocation, which contains a historical provider factor based on 2006/07 delivery.
Achievement funding 25% for Train to Gain and 25% (excluding key skills and technical certificate) for Apprenticeships.	Retention and achievement funding accounted for by the success factor within the provider factor (see page 36).
Withdrawal may impact on funding as payment based on monthly instalments.	Funding not reduced if learner is withdrawn after minimum attendance period (see page 48).
Funding claims made every fourth working day of the month.	Funding claims submitted five times (minimum).
Fee element (funding deducted) is weighted by the provider factor and the employer contributes.	Fee element is not weighted by the provider factor and learner pays the fee (see page 46).
No transitional protection, except for NVQs that were previously FE.	Transitional protection applied to funding rate.
Three programme weightings (excluding technical certificates).	Seven programme weightings.
Limited number of eligible qualifications.	Wide variety of eligible qualifications.
All funding rates listed as SLNs.	Some rates unlisted and listed rates are SLN glh (see page 32).
The learner's workplace defines area cost uplift. Disadvantage uplift ineligible for Train to Gain.	The provider's main site defines area cost uplift and disadvantage uplift eligible for all enrolments.
No per learner cap on funding.	Annual per learner cap of 1.75 SLN.
Providers can request more than the indicative maximum allocation from regional response fund.	Little ability to earn more than allocation. Any increase is likely to be limited to adults, where affordable.

The formula

The 2008/09 funding methodology brings with it new terminology and a significantly different way of calculating funding.

To quote the Learning and Skills Council (LSC):

> 'The move to a demand-led funding system in 2008/09 signifies a wholesale step change for the learning and skills sector.'
>
> www.lsc.gov.uk

Central to this demand-led funding system is a new formula. The formula is used to calculate enrolment, learner and allocation funding values for all three of the new funding models described in the previous chapter. It will therefore be of interest to all LSC-funded post-16 providers (FE colleges, school sixth forms and all other providers) as well as those with an interest in LSC funding. In fact, even schools with no intention of creating a sixth form should take note, as the Government might extend the formula to 14- and 15-year-old funding from 2011/12. Perhaps the formula will be all that is left to remind us of the LSC – if, as currently planned, it is abolished.

Note

A minority of LSC funding in the FE system will not use the demand-led formula in 2008/09. These include Adult Safeguarded Learning (ASL), Offender Learning and Skills Service (OLASS), Skills for Jobs (SfJ) and European Social Fund (ESF) funding.

This chapter looks at the application of the formula, starting with an introduction to the formula and then in turn exploring each element in more detail. Perhaps the most important element to understand is the Standard Learner Number (SLN), a new unweighted volume measure for valuing every learner, enrolment and qualification. Planning delivery to generate sufficient SLNs will be crucial, and it is arguably the only element of the formula over which providers will have significant control.

Finally, before you progress into the chapter, it is worth remembering that this national formula is designed to generate appropriate funding for a diverse range of providers, learners, qualifications and circumstances. Therefore, while the new formula is arguably simpler than the previous formulas, it remains complex. Three funding-formula consultations between 2005 and 2007 have brought us to this point, and simplicity versus accuracy is likely to continue to be an area of significant debate.

Accuracy (sometimes referred to as fairness)

Introduction to the demand-led formula

The demand-led formula has been introduced for 2008/09 to resolve two criticisms of the previous funding formula: complexity and incompatibility.

Simplification: The new demand-led funding formula is designed to be simpler for all those involved to understand and operate.

Compatibility: The funding formula is used within the 16–18, adult learner-responsive and employer-responsive funding models. For the first time, school sixth forms use the same formula as FE colleges, and the Government might extend the formula to the whole 14–19 phase by 2011/12.

The demand-led funding formula for each enrolment is as follows:

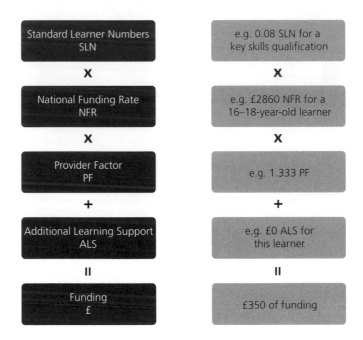

This formula is used not only for each enrolment, but also to allocate funding for the 2008/09 academic year (01/08/08 to 31/07/09). For example:

3000 SLN x £2860 NFR x 1.333 PF + £1m ALS = £12.4m allocation

In the example above, the provider is allocated £12.4m, and in order to achieve this allocation they will have to deliver 3000 Standard Learner Numbers and spend £1m of Additional Learning Support. In-year the provider cannot influence the national funding rate, nor can they influence the provider factor in the 16–18 and adult leaner-responsive funding model.

Simplification

The new funding formula is certainly simple at first glance. However, it should come as no surprise that a national funding formula that is capable of paying appropriate sums to any learner type, on any course and at any location in England is inevitably complex. In fact, many of the features from the previous FE mainstream funding formula have been adapted to continue working within the new demand-led formula.

From the old FE formula	to the new demand-led formula
National Base Rates	Standard Learner Number for course multiplied by the national funding rate
16–18 minimum funding guarantee uplift	The new 16–18 national funding rate includes the 16–18 uplift
Programme weighting, disadvantage uplift and area costs uplift	All three are included in the 2008/09 provider factor, and are derived from a provider's 2006/07 weighted average
Success for all factor	Not included
Specialist-institution factor	New 1.92 (G) programme weighting for land-based programmes
Tri-annual census dates and achievement factor	Minimum attendance period and success factor within the provider factor
Assumed Fee Income	Fee element (42.5% in 2008/09)
Entry funding element within National Base Rates	Short programme modifier within the provider factor
Loadbanded base rates	Unlisted Standard Learner Numbers
Tri-annual taper and maximum funding per learner	1.75 Standard Learner Number cap per learner per year (16–18 and adult learner-responsive funding models only)

Compatibility

A common formula for schools and colleges brings significant advantages, particularly in terms of harmonising the funding rates, sharing data systems, comparing performance and being partners in diploma delivery. However, compatibility with the employer-responsive funding model is limited by the desire to fund based on actual delivery. Therefore, any simplification associated with a historical provider factor cannot be realised. This will be welcomed by those that argue that simplification reduces accuracy.

Standard Learner Numbers

The Standard Learner Number (SLN) is a new volume measure that replaces the National Base Rate as the first element in the funding formula:

$$\textbf{SLN} \times NFR \times PF + ALS = Funding$$

Every enrolment has an SLN Value, which is either set by the LSC (listed), or determined by the actual course duration (unlisted). The LSC publishes 16–18 and adult learner-responsive SLN Values as guided learning hours (glh), called SLN glh. To convert an SLN glh into an SLN it is divided by 450.

$$\frac{SLN\ glh}{450} = SLN$$

Guided learning hours are the hours of learning activity with a tutor or trainer. Therefore, SLN glh and SLNs are a measure of duration, which is considered a key determinant of cost and therefore relative funding. SLNs are assigned to an academic year, based on the start and end dates, and enrolments are added together to create a learner-level SLN. In the 16–18 and adult learner-responsive funding models the SLN is capped at 1.75 per learner per year.

Note

The LSC publishes a number of qualification SLN Values within its *2008/09 Funding Rates* document. However, comprehensive and up-to-date listed (and unlisted) SLN Values can be found in the LSC's online Learning Aim Database (LAD) at: http://providers.lsc.gov.uk/lad

Listed SLNs

The LSC lists SLN glh values for qualifications that have a relatively common duration across the sector. The SLN glh will either be listed on the basis of a recommendation by an awarding body, or LSC analysis of the glh used by providers in previous years. The listed value represents a price for delivering the qualification, regardless of the duration actually planned by the provider. In the case of school sixth forms, all SLN Values are listed.

The table on the following page lists a typical first-year A-level programme for a learner in the 16–18 funding model. All the SLN Values are listed, so if the provider recorded and delivered different durations this would not alter the SLN Values, nor the funding. Also, the learner SLN total of 1.75 is equal to the annual 1.75 SLN cap, so any additional enrolments would reduce the SLN Value of all the enrolments such that the total could not exceed 1.75. The reference to 'daytime' is important, as A-levels and GCSEs have a lower rate when taught in the evening (*see pages 64 and 66*).

Sep '08 – Jul '09 daytime delivery	SLN glh	SLN
AS Economics	150	0.333
AS History	150	0.333
AS Politics	150	0.333
AS English	150	0.333
AS General Studies	36	0.08
Key skill in numeracy	36	0.08
Entitlement (including tutorial)	114	0.253
Total per learner	786	1.747

Unlisted SLNs

Unlisted SLNs describe those enrolments for which the LSC has not listed an SLN Value, as a common duration has not been identified. In these cases, the SLN glh is the enrolment duration as recorded by the provider. For example, a Certificate in Adult Literacy taught for 90 glh within the adult learner-responsive funding model would have an unlisted SLN Value of 0.2. Unlisted SLNs are almost exclusively within the adult learner-responsive model.

Example of unlisted SLNs, which replace the complex loadbands

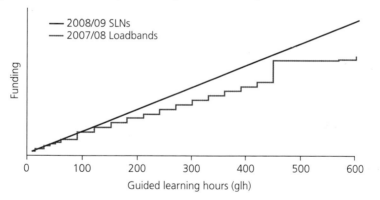

The key change has been to replace glh bands with a straight divisor method. This brings a significant degree of simplification, as now every glh has the same value of 0.00222r SLN (one divided by 450). It also helpfully removes the incentive to plan courses with a glh at the bottom of a band.

Note

It is important to recognise the difference between annual SLNs and full-time equivalents (FTEs). Firstly, learners can account for up to 1.75 SLN each, so many providers will have more SLNs than learners or FTEs. Secondly, listed SLNs (unlike FTEs) are not determined by actual delivery; their value is set nationally each year by the LSC.

National and transitional funding rates

In December 2007 the LSC published the 2008/09 national funding rates (NFR) for further education. These rates convert SLNs into an unweighted funding value within the demand-led funding formula:

$$SLN \times \mathbf{NFR} \times PF + ALS = Funding$$

In 2008/09 there are three different rates across the funding models. The school sixth form rate of £2945 is 3% greater than the 16–18 college and Apprenticeship rate of £2860, which is 3% greater than the adult learner and employer rate of £2775.

For example, the unweighted funding for a Key Skill would be:

Funding model	Funding for key skills qualification
16–18 school sixth forms	0.08 SLN x £2945 NFR = £235.60
16–18 colleges	0.08 SLN x £2860 NFR = £228.80
16–18 Apprenticeships	0.08 SLN x £2860 NFR = £228.80
Adult learner-responsive	0.08 SLN x £2775 NFR = £222.00
Employer-responsive	0.08 SLN x £2775 NFR = £222.00

National funding rates will be published each year, and are likely to change to take account of inflation and affordability.

2008/09 National funding rates and increase from 2007/08

Funding model	National funding rate	Increase
16–18 school sixth forms	£2945	2.1%
16–18 colleges	£2860	2.1%
16–18 Apprenticeships	£2860	1.6%
Adult learner-responsive	£2775	1.5%
Employer-responsive	£2775	1.5%

Note

In this new national funding formula, it is easy to confuse qualification rates with national rates. This is because in 2007/08 qualifications had cash National Base Rates. For 2008/09 qualification cash base rates have been converted into SLNs, so need to be multiplied by the new national funding rate before they can be described in cash. So qualification rates (SLNs) and national rates (£) are no longer the same thing.

There are only three different national funding rates in 2008/09. However, some providers will be set a transitional rate that could be higher or lower than the national rate. The transitional rate is designed to dampen the impact of moving from the current funding formula to the new demand-led formula. All other things being equal, some providers will significantly benefit from the new formula, so they will be set a transitional rate lower than the national rate. Conversely, those who lose out to the new formula will be set a rate higher than the national rate. The rate is known as transitional because each year the LSC will alter the rate so that over time all providers converge onto the national rates.

The LSC calculates the value of transitional rates by comparing providers' 2006/07 data under the current and the new funding formula. In the 16–18 model, if the provider gains or loses by more than 2.1% under the new funding formula (after inflation), then a transitional rate is calculated to cap the gain or loss at 2.1%.

Although the transitional rate is provider-specific, like the national rate it is applied to all delivery in the funding model to which it relates.

Transitional protection in action (example)

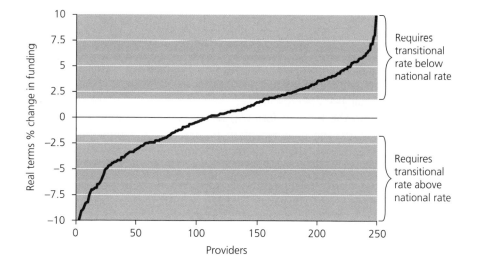

The provider factor

The provider factor is calculated individually for each provider and funding model, and is designed to reflect the relative costs of delivery, costs associated with certain groups of learners, and quality. It is the 'weighting' that sits within the funding formula for every enrolment and allocation:

$$\text{SLN} \times \text{NFR} \times \textbf{PF} + \text{ALS} = \text{Funding}$$

The provider factor is calculated by multiplying five elements together. The table below lists these elements with example values.

Provider factor elements	16–18 model	Adult learner-responsive funding model
Programme weighting	1.215	1.257
Disadvantage uplift	1.077	1.075
Area costs uplift	1.200	1.200
Short programme modifier	1.000	1.017
Success factor	0.849	0.855
Example provider factors	**1.333**	**1.410**

Like the national and transitional funding rates, the provider factor is set by the LSC for all enrolments in a given funding model. For 2008/09 it has been calculated by the LSC from full-year 2006/07 funding data. This means it is applying historical information within the funding formula, which will bring simplification at the expense of accuracy. The only exception to this rule is within the employer-responsive funding model, where the historical provider factor is used only for the purposes of setting maximum contract values. Actual funding generated within the employer-responsive funding model will include elements of the provider factor, but they will be calculated individually for each and every enrolment.

Note

While the provider factors are set once each year for each model, it is worth understanding the five elements. Remember: what providers deliver in 2008/09 will determine the provider factor used in 2010/11.

The **programme weighting** in the 2008/09 provider factor is a weighted average from actual delivery in 2006/07. Programme weightings recognise that some programmes are more costly to deliver than others. In 2008/09 the 16–18 and adult learner-responsive funding models will have seven weightings, while the adult employer-responsive funding model will have three.

Programme weighting for 16–18 and adult learner-responsive funding models		
A	1	e.g. NVQ in Business and Administration
B	1.12	e.g. NVQ in Health and Social Care
C	1.3	e.g. NVQ in Beauty Therapy
D	1.6	e.g. NVQ in Performing Engineering Operations
E	1.72	e.g. NVQ in Agriculture Management
F	1.4	Basic skills specific (e.g. Level 1 Numeracy)
G	1.92	Replaces specialist college factor for some qualifications and providers in the agriculture and horticulture sector
Programme weighting for employer-responsive funding model		
A	1	e.g. NVQ in Business and Administration
J	1.25	e.g. NVQ in Beauty Therapy
K	1.5	e.g. NVQ in Performing Engineering Operations

The **disadvantage uplift** is designed to compensate providers for higher costs associated with disadvantaged learners. Learners can qualify for an 8 to 32% uplift, based on their home postcode, or for other reasons listed by the LSC, such as a 12% uplift if classed as a basic-skills learner.

The **area costs uplift** is designed to compensate providers in the south-east of England for higher costs associated with their location. It rises to a maximum of 20% within Inner London, and the only change for 2008/09 is within the employer-responsive funding model, where it will be calculated for each enrolment according to the delivery location, not the location of the provider.

The **short-programme modifier** is new in 2008/09, and is designed to recognise the slightly higher set-up costs for short courses below 225 glh. The shorter the programme, the higher the short-programme modifier:

The **success factor** is also new for 2008/09, and adjusts funding for learners who drop out and/or do not achieve their qualification. The success factor is the mid-point between the provider's weighted average success rate and 100 per cent:

$$\text{Short-programme modifier} = \left(0.3 \times \frac{225 - \text{learner glh}}{225}\right)$$

The employer-responsive funding model funds retention and achievement separately. Hence the provider factor used to set maximum contract values includes a retention and achievement factor, rather than a success factor.

$$\text{Success factor} = 0.5 + \frac{\text{Weighted average success rate}}{2}$$

Additional Learning Support

Additional Learning Support (ALS) is funding within the three models for additional activities that provide direct learning support to learners. For example, it may pay for a communication support worker or additional tutor support. ALS is added as the final element in the demand-led formula.

$$\text{SLN} \times \text{NFR} \times \text{PF} + \textbf{ALS} = \text{Funding}$$

The way that ALS is recorded for 2008/09 in the 16–18 and adult learner-responsive funding models is much the same as in 2007/08, and detailed information can be found in the LSC's *Funding Compliance Advice and Audit Guidance 2008/09*.
- The minimum ALS claim for a full-time learner is £501.
- The minimum ALS claim for a part-time learner is £170.
- ALS costs form (below £5500) to be used for low-level claims.
- ALS costs form (above £5500) to be used for high-level claims.
- Claims above £19,000 need to be LSC 'approved in principle'.

However, the way ALS funding is allocated in 2008/09 has changed significantly. A formula has been introduced to calculate low-level ALS allocations, and school sixth forms have been allocated ALS funding for the first time using this formula. Low-level allocations account for approximately 95% of learners accessing ALS, and 65% of the ALS budget.

Note

While the formula is being introduced only for low-level ALS allocations, this simply means it only applies to ALS claimed at a rate of less than £5500 per learner. Many providers have low-level ALS claims in excess of a million pounds, so any change to the allocation method should be of significant interest for 2008/09 and beyond.

The formula for the 16–18 and adult learner-responsive ALS allocations are based on provider delivery in 2006/07 and are complex and different. However, each formula is designed in such a way that the lower the prior attainment or levels of study, the higher the ALS allocation.

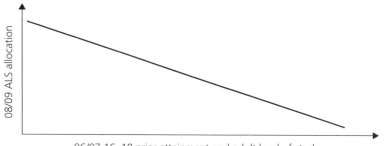

06/07 16–18 prior attainment and adult level of study

To determine the 16–18 funding model ALS allocations for both colleges and school sixth forms, the LSC has matched 2006/07 provider data with nationally held GCSE points scores for English and mathematics. A formula is then applied to these scores to ensure that the lower the scores (prior attainment), the higher the ALS allocation.

Prior attainment data is not robust enough to use for adults, so the level of studying in 2006/07 is used in a formula to determine the 2008/09 ALS allocations. As the previous diagram illustrated, the lower the average level of study in 2006/07, the higher the ALS allocation will be in 2008/09.

The LSC recognises that the introduction of a formula will not only allocate ALS to providers who have never had allocations in the past, but will also impact on providers with ALS allocations, some considerably. Therefore, colleges with existing ALS will be allocated 60% of the 2008/09 allocation using the formula, and the remaining 40% will be negotiated with the LSC. However, this is still likely to alter some allocations significantly and the negotiated percentage is likely to fall below 40% after 2008/09.

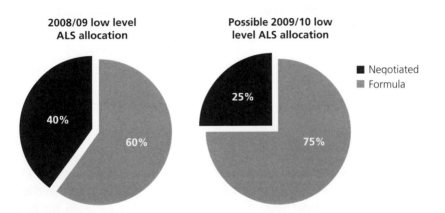

Note

Additional Learning Support (ALS) should not be confused with Learner Support Funding (LSF). ALS is within the funding models and pays for supporting the learning (such as dyslexia support). LSF is not part of the new funding models and as in previous years, pays for supporting the learner (such as paying for childcare).

The ALS for Apprenticeships in 2008/09 within the employer-responsive funding model differs very little from the arrangements in 2007/08. The ALS for Apprenticeships consists of Additional Learning Needs (ALN) funding to support numeracy and literacy and/or Additional Social Needs (ASN) funding to support emotional, behavioural or motivational difficulties. As a result, ALS for Apprenticeships is also referred to as Additional Learning and Support Needs (ALSN). The LSC does not anticipate that Train to Gain learners will access ALN or ASN, except in exceptional circumstances.

Madeup College (worked example)

It may come as no surprise that Madeup College is a wholly fictional further education institution. Madeup College receives funding from all three funding models, and only exists in these two pages as an attempt to provide useful worked examples at allocation level.

In order to calculate the various formula-based allocations for Madeup College, it is necessary to set the four values, four times, within the formula.

1. Standard Learner Numbers (SLN)   Negotiated with LSC
2. National or Transitional Rate (NFR)   Non-negotiable
3. Provider factor (PF)   Non-negotiable
4. Additional Learning Support (ALS)   40% negotiated with LSC

These four values, four times, for Madeup College are as follows:

Funding model	SLN	NFR	PF	ALS
16–18 (excl. Apprenticeships)	3000	£2860	1.333	£1m
16–18 Apprenticeships	200	£2860	1.486	£0
Employer-responsive	400	£2775	1.435	£0
Adult learner-responsive	2000	£2775	1.410	£1m

Madeup College does not require any transitional funding rates. However, 500 of the 2000 adult learner-responsive funding model SLNs are for learners who are expected to pay fees. This means the funding allocation is reduced by £589,688 for the fee element, which is equal to value that the LSC 'assumes' will be collected as a fee from the learner (500 x £2775 x 42.5%). *See page 46* for further information on the fee element.

Therefore, once the formula SLN x NFR x PF + ALS has been applied (and £589,688 has been deducted from the adult learner-responsive total) Madeup College has funding allocations for 2008/09 totalling £23m.

Funding model	Provision	ALS	Total
16–18 (excl. Apprenticeships)	£11,437,140	£1m	£12,437,140
16–18 Apprenticeships	£849,992	£0	£849,992
Employer-responsive	£1,592,850	£0	£1,592,850
Adult learner-responsive	£7,235,813	£1m	£8,235,813
Total	£21,115,795	£2m	£23,115,795

Formula funding of £23m for 2008/09 at Madeup College:

16–18 funding model (excl. Apprenticeships) Allocation of £12.4m, of which £1m is Additional Learning Support. Actual delivery unlikely to alter the funding received but will be considered for 2009/10 allocation.

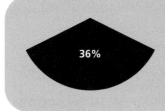

Employer-responsive funding model
16–18 Apprenticeship allocation of £0.8m with employer model rules.

Adult allocation of £1.6m consists of Apprenticeships and Train to Gain funding, which is paid on delivery.

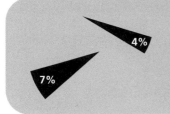

Adult learner-responsive funding model
Allocation of £8.2m, of which £1m is Additional Learning Support. The LSC has also set Madeup College tuition fee targets of £590k and based on performance may alter the allocation in-year.

Note

FE mainstream funding has been replaced by separate 16–18 and adult learner-responsive funding models, so it is no longer possible to move funding between age cohorts. In other words, if providers do not achieve 16–18 funding targets, this can no longer be offset by exceeding adult funding targets. This is because the 16–18 and adult budgets now sit within two government departments, the DCSF (16–18) and DIUS (adult).

While Madeup College has been given a £23m allocation, they need to plan sufficient provision in each of the models to achieve this funding target. For example, if all their 16–18-year-old non-Apprenticeship learners studied a programme with an SLN Value of 1.75, they would need to plan to enrol at least 1715 learners to meet the £11.4m funding target (3000 SLN divided by 1.75 SLN per learner). However, learners do not all study for the same qualifications or follow the same programme durations. There are many thousands of qualifications available for formula funding within one or all of the three models. The following two sections cover learner issues and the history, purpose and funding for a number of popular qualifications.

The learners

This chapter covers four important funding rules for learners:

Eligibility

Some learners and courses are ineligible for LSC funding, so it is vital before planning a course or enrolling a learner that the eligibility criteria have been met. This section summarises who is and who is not eligible for LSC funding, as well as the types of evidence and records that need to be kept in order to justify the funding claim. It also lists the types of courses that are ineligible for LSC funding. However, eligibility is a complex area and it is always advisable to refer to the detailed eligibility guidance published by the LSC. The LSC also has some discretion in this area, so if in doubt or seeking a solution it is always best to contact them.

Fee element

Many adult learners are ineligble for fee-remission funding, which means the funding is reduced by a fee element. This section summarises how the fee element has risen in recent years to almost double the level in 2004/05, which may explain why some providers' tuition fees have risen so fast. The formula for the fee-element deduction within the learner (unweighted) and employer (weighted) funding models is then explained. Finally, the 'co-funded rate', which is simply the funding rate for adults not receiving fee remission funding, and formula are explained.

Minimum attendance

Learners need to pass a minimum attendance period before they can be defined as a start, generate funding and count towards targets. There are three minimum attendance periods in the new funding methodology used in all three funding models. This section describes these periods, along with the definitions of start dates, planned end dates and, perhaps most importantly in this context, the withdrawal date (last date of attendance). This counting methodology is quite different from previous methods, which included fixed census dates. In terms of full-time learners, the significance of this is looked at in detail, as withdrawals in October may no longer generate funding nor count towards targets.

SLN per learner ratio

The LSC is keen on ratios as it uses them to make comparisons between providers and consider value for money, and as a basis for negotiating future funding allocations. This section looks at a new ratio called the SLN per learner ratio (or simply 'SLN ratio'), which the LSC is using as part of the new funding methodology. Since SLNs are an unweighted unit of cost for the LSC, it is keen to avoid the average cost of learners (SLN per learner) rising. The aim is to keep public spending under control and stop providers from expanding learners' programme size, which would increase the SLN per learner ratio. However, this section considers evidence that suggests the SLN per learner ratio will inevitably rise as a consequence of providers altering their mix and balance of provision to deliver government targets and LSC priority provision.

Eligibility

Not all courses, nor all learners, are eligible for LSC funding. Therefore, before planning a course or enrolling a learner, it is important that providers establish whether they are eligible. The LSC funding guidance, available at www.lsc.gov.uk, contains the detailed eligibility rules.

It can be difficult to determine whether a learner or course is eligible for LSC funding, so it is always recommended that providers:
- identify a member of staff as the eligibility expert, who keeps up to date with the rules, evidence and audit requirements;
- consult the LSC on a case-by-case basis when in doubt;
- consult the LSC if they believe that an ineligible learner or course should be considered for funding in exceptional circumstances.

Learner eligibility

The following summarises *just some* of the learner eligibility rules, but providers should always consult the detailed LSC guidance.

Eligible for LSC funding	Ineligible for LSC funding
'Home' learners with 'ordinary residence' for 3 years preceding academic year (defined by LSC)	'Overseas' learners, who are defined as not meeting the 'home' learner criteria
Asylum seekers legally in the UK	Person subject to deportation order
Those above 'compulsory school age' and resident in England	Those of 'compulsory school age' or resident outside England
Those enrolled on a Level 4 or 5 course not funded by HEFCE	Those currently enrolled on a higher-education course funded by HEFCE
Provider employees studying outside working hours, plus basic skills provision in working hours	Provider employees studying in working hours (except basic qualifications for teachers or trainers, which are eligible)
Full-time learners enrolled with one provider at any given time	Those LSC funded as full-time learners at another provider
All learners detained in prison	

Course eligibility

In order to claim LSC funding, providers are required to maintain records of learner existence and eligibility. The LSC outlines the detailed requirements within its funding guidance, which as a minimum include signed records of:

- learning agreements;
- enrolment forms;
- learner records of attendance;
- achievement evidence.

In order to claim funding for courses, providers must send enrolment information to the LSC as data within an Individualised Learner Record (ILR). Each enrolment requires an eight-digit code known as the learning aim, which identifies the course the learner is enrolled on. Only those learning aims that are eligible for LSC funding can be submitted within an ILR claim. Therefore, when planning a course it is advisable to first check eligibility using the Learning Aim Database (LAD) (http://providers.lsc.gov.uk/).

When planning a course, the LAD can also be used to help determine:

- the listed SLN or SLN glh funding rates;
- the programme weighting for the learner or employer model;
- whether the qualification contributes to government targets;
- whether the enrolment may be eligible for automatic fee remission.

Learner, course and enrolment data: path to eligible funding

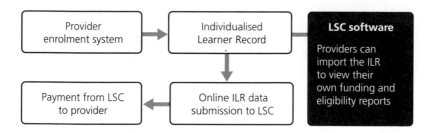

Provision ineligible for LSC funding includes:

- vendor-certificated qualifications (e.g. Microsoft);
- courses of fewer than nine guided learning hours, except for adults when the qualification is on the National Qualification Framework (NQF);
- additional or optional units beyond the minimum required;
- single units outside the Qualification and Credit Framework (QCF);
- company-specific knowledge courses;
- courses for 16–18-year-olds not approved under section 96;
- qualification re-sits and stand-alone courses designed to meet employers' statutory or other responsibilities.

The fee element and the co-funded rate

Many adult learners, particularly those who are employed, are ineligible for full funding because it is 'assumed' they will pay tuition fees. In 2008/09 the LSC will reduce the full funding by 42.5% of the unweighted (adult learner-responsive funding model) or weighted (employer-responsive funding model) funding. In the previous funding formula, this reduction was called the Assumed Fee Income (AFI), and in the new funding formula it is known as the fee element. The fee element percentage has been rising year on year since 2004/05.

Rising fee element (funding deducted for fee payers)

Academic year	2004/05	2005/06	2006/07	2007/08	2008/09
Unweighted full time base rate	£2394	£2513	£2576	£2640	£2775
Fee element %	25%	27.5%	32.5%	37.5%	42.5%
Fee element £	£599	£691	£837	£990	£1179
Annual increase %		15%	21%	18%	19%
Annual increase £		£93	£146	£153	£189

As shown in the table above, the fee element has nearly doubled over the last four years, which means that not only has the funding reduction doubled, but also that providers' tuition fees would have to double to maintain overall income levels. The LSC can and do set total tuition fee income targets based on the fee deduction, but they cannot dictate the individual tuition fees that providers set as this would fall foul of competition law.

The fee element formula differs in each adult funding model

Learner fee element = SLN glh / 450 x funding rate x 42.5%

Employer fee element = SLN x £2775 x provider factor x 42.5%

Adult learner-responsive funding model

The table below contains an example fee element using the national funding rate of £2775. In the adult learner-responsive funding model, the calculation is unweighted (excludes the provider factor), so the fee element would be the same for all providers, regardless of, for example, location.

Example enrolment	Fee element (adult learner-responsive funding model)
Full-time NVQ with listed SLN glh of 520	520 / 450 x £2775 x 42.5% = £1363

The fee element can also be calculated on the basis of £2.62 per SLN glh.

The co-funded rate is another new term, which is important as it is the rate that is applied to fee-paying adult SLNs instead of the full funding rate (national or transitional). It is calculated as follows:

> Co-funded rate = funding rate – (funding rate x 42.5% / provider factor)

The total funding for fee-paying adults is then calculated as follows:

> Co-funded funding = SLN x co-funded rate x provider factor

Note

If a provider has a transitional funding rate, this should be used instead of the £2775 national rate to calculate the fee element and co-funded rate. However, the LSC fee targets are based on the national rate, so providers could face criticism if they set their fees according to the transitional rate (although the fee remains a provider-based decision).

Employer-responsive funding model

Calculating the fee element (or 'contribution') to be deducted from adult employer-funding is much simpler, as there are no transitional funding rates, and the fee element is always 42.5% of the full (weighted) funding.

Example enrolment	Fee element (employer-responsive funding model)
NVQ Level 2 (higher rate)	0.429 x £2775 x provider factor x 42.5%

Note

The Apprenticeship fee element percentage will be in the region of 42.5%, but is actually listed within the Learning Aims Database (LAD) for each individual element within the Apprenticeship Framework.

Minimum attendance

Minimum attendance is also referred to as 'the definition of a start' or 'when they count'. In funding terms, it is the minimum duration of on-programme learning activities required for funding to be claimed. If the learner withdraws from the enrolment before this minimum period, then funding cannot be claimed, nor can the learner be counted towards LSC targets.

The minimum attendance rules are the same across all three funding models, as described in the table below.

Course duration	Minimum attendance
24 weeks or more	6 weeks
2 to 24 weeks	2 weeks
Less than two weeks	1 attendance

The course duration is based on the number of calendar days between the start date and planned end date of the enrolment. The attendance duration is then measured by the distance between the start date and the actual end date. Therefore, if the attendance duration is less than the minimum attendance, funding will not be generated.

Note

The withdrawal date is the last date of attendance, as recorded on the enrolment register. It is not the date the learner informs the provider they will not be participating, nor a given period such as four weeks after the final attendance, nor the date when the data is changed.

The diagram below highlights the three minimum attendance periods for a one-week, 18-week and full-year course. In these examples, all the courses start in the first term, when the first learning activity typically takes place in the middle of September.

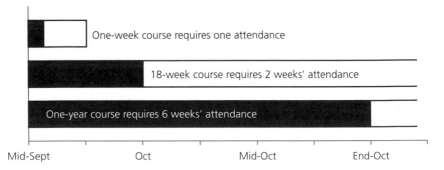

Within the 16–18 and adult learner-responsive funding models, once the minimum attendance period has been achieved, the provider can claim all the funding. Within the employer-responsive funding model, the minimum attendance rules are the same, but monthly instalments only continue while the learner is on-programme and 25% is held back for payment on achievement.

In the 16–18 and adult learner-responsive funding models, if an enrolment spans two academic years, then a second minimum attendance period must be passed (starting from 1 August in the second year). Failure to pass this second period means the annualised funding cannot be claimed for the second year.

For example, a full-time two-year course such as the BTEC National Diploma might begin on 1 August in 2008/09 and end on 31 July 2009/10. The learner would need to attend until at least six weeks into the second year (middle of September 2009) for full funding to be claimed.

| 1st | 6 weeks | | 2nd | 6 weeks |

Aug 08   Aug 09

The example above is relatively simple because the course starts in August and finishes in July, so the funding is exactly 50% for each year (excluding inflation). In reality, courses of this nature usually start in the middle of September, so the funding split is unlikely to be exactly 50% for each year.

Note

Many courses in the second year begin in mid-September. If a learner withdraws during the summer, the withdrawal date may be incorrectly recorded as the start of the second year, and all of the funding will be claimed. Providers need to be particularly careful to avoid this.

This new definition of a start is significantly different from previous ones. For example, in further education it has until now been based on learners passing one of three funding census dates (1 October, 1 February and 15 May). Therefore, traditional full-time learners starting in the middle of September now have a six-week minimum attendance period, four more weeks than in 2007/08.

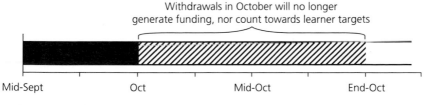

Withdrawals in October will no longer
generate funding, nor count towards learner targets

Mid-Sept   Oct   Mid-Oct   End-Oct

Caution is therefore advised when setting 2008/09 targets or making learner number comparisons based on previous counting methodologies.

SLN per learner ratio

Ratios are important, as they are used by the LSC to make judgements about the relative costs of provision and to inform allocations and targets. In the past, funding per full-time equivalent (FTE) was a popular ratio with the LSC, but it was not without its critics who highlighted that:

- FTEs are not well understood, nor does the funding per FTE ratio take account of learner participation;
- FTEs are based on actual glh, which was a problem for the workplace NVQs as they have relatively few glh;
- funding per FTE includes weightings, so a rising ratio might simply be a result of increased success rates.

The new funding formula has unweighted Standard Learner Numbers (SLN), which presented the opportunity to introduce a new ratio. The SLN per learner ratio is likely to become an increasingly important measure, as it describes the average unweighted value of each learner. Put simply, the higher the ratio, the fewer learners can share the same pot of funding. This is important, and the LSC has stated in *Our Statement of Priorities – Better Skills, Better Jobs, Better Lives,* LSC (November 2007) that 'to offer opportunities for as many learners as possible we need to control unit cost increases, including those arising from the expansion of learners' programmes'. The example below shows how the ratio might rise.

Programme	SLN	Programme	SLN
BTEC First Diploma	1	BTEC First Diploma	1
One key skill	0.08	Two key skills	0.16
SLN per learner ratio	1.08	SLN per learner ratio	1.16

A provider delivering larger programmes to the same learners is perhaps the most obvious reason for an increase in the SLN per learner ratio. In the example above, the ratio has increased by 7% from 1.08 to 1.16, simply by delivering an additional key skills qualification.

This approach is naturally unpopular with the LSC, particularly as its funds are limited and it wants to reverse the decline in adult participation. The LSC response would probably be to cap the SLN per learner ratio when negotiating funding allocations. However, the average value of both 16–18 and adult learners has been rising for a number of years, and is likely to continue to do so for the foreseeable future. The available evidence suggests that this rise is less to do with providers expanding learners' programmes, and more to do with the Government's prioritisation of funding for both higher-value full-time 16–18-year-olds and target-bearing adults.

16–18 full-time growth with part-time reductions

In recent years, the LSC has taken the focus off very different trends in full- and part-time participation by setting only total participation targets. Although total participation may not change, full-time learners are increasing as part-time learners are decreasing (probably as a by-product of the cut in adult short course funding described below). As a result, the average learner value (SLN per learner ratio) will inevitably increase. This is demonstrated in the table below, with actual LSC projected learners and some example SLN per learner ratios, which remain constant for full-timers (1.5) and part-timers (0.5), yet increase year on year when combined.

LSC projected learners		2008/09	2009/10	2010/11
16–18 full-time	learners ('000)	660	664	666
16–18 part-time	learners ('000)	113	109	107
Total	learners ('000)	773	773	773

Example SLNs		2008/09	2009/10	2010/11
16–18 full-time	SLN per learner	1.5	1.5	1.5
16–18 part-time	SLN per learner	0.5	0.5	0.5
Total	SLN per learner	1.354	1.359	1.362

Adults on increasingly higher value and priority qualifications

Although overall investment in adult provision has remained relatively stable, a stark consequence of the Government's prioritisation of adult funding towards skills has been a significant overall reduction in adult learners. The reason for this was candidly described and predicted by the Government in October 2005:

> We are broadly maintaining the overall public funding that the LSC will be able to allocate to support adult learning but the pattern of that learning will change. To meet our national priorities, we need to shift the pattern so that we provide longer and more expensive courses for adults. So while maintaining the overall volume of adult funding, we estimate there will be a net reduction in publicly-funded places of around 230,000 (about 6%).
>
> Source: *LSC Grant Letter 2006–07*, DFES (October 2005)

For example, a provider could fund 1000 learners on low-priority short courses with an SLN per learner ratio of 0.1 **or** 200 learners on a priority first full Level 2 with an SLN per learner ratio of 0.5. Therefore, as providers alter their mix and balance to deliver government targets, the average value of the learner (SLN per learner ratio) will increase, often substantially.

The provision

The next few chapters look in detail at funding rates and related issues for some of the most popular qualifications and learning programmes.

For the purposes of clarity and ease of use, this chapter has been split into five sub-chapters, each containing a number of qualifications and programmes that have a common theme. The aim is that they can be used as a reference guide for those staff involved in the planning and delivery of this provision, and as such it contains diagrams and worked examples.

Each section covers the listed and unlisted rates as published by the LSC within the online Learning Aim Database (LAD) and funding rates guidance document. These are either SLN glh, or SLNs in the case of the Apprenticeship Framework element and NVQs in the workplace. There are many qualifications that are not covered in this chapter, but their rates will also be within the LAD, and the national formula remains the same.

To determine the financial value of the SLN glh, it must first be divided by 450 to convert it into an SLN rate. It is then multiplied by the relevant national funding rate to express the unweighted funding value. Providers wishing to convert this into weighted funding would need to apply the elements of their provider factor from the relevant funding model. To make it more qualification specific, a recalculated provider factor could include, for example, the programme weighting for the specific qualification. However, funding generated during the year within the 16–18 and adult learner-responsive funding models will always apply the single historical provider factor (*see page 36*).

In the case of the employer-responsive funding model, most rates are listed by the LSC as SLNs rather than SLN glh. The SLNs are multiplied by the relevant national funding rate to express the unweighted funding value. The enrolment-specific elements of the provider factor would then need to be applied to determine the weighted funding, which is paid in-year.

Note

In all cases, the SLN Values have been listed to three decimal places. However, for the purposes of accuracy, the calculation for unweighted funding has been applied with many more decimal places within a spreadsheet. See page 108 for further explanation.

Skills for Life provision

Skills for Life was introduced in 2001 as a national strategy for improving adult basic skills in numeracy and literacy (including ESOL), following the Moser report on basic skills in 2000. The original Public Service Agreement (PSA) target was for 2.25 million adults to achieve a Skills for Life qualification at Entry Level 3 to Level 2 by 2010. This target remains, but as a consequence of the *Leitch Review of Skills,* HM Treasury (December 2006) in 2006, a new target extends this to 95% of adults achieving literacy at Level 1 and numeracy at Entry Level 3 by 2020. Therefore these qualifications are a high priority for the Government (particularly at target-bearing levels). Skills for Life provision can be delivered stand-alone, or as GCSEs and key skills within larger programmes, often alongside the 16–18 entitlement. (*See page 60.*)

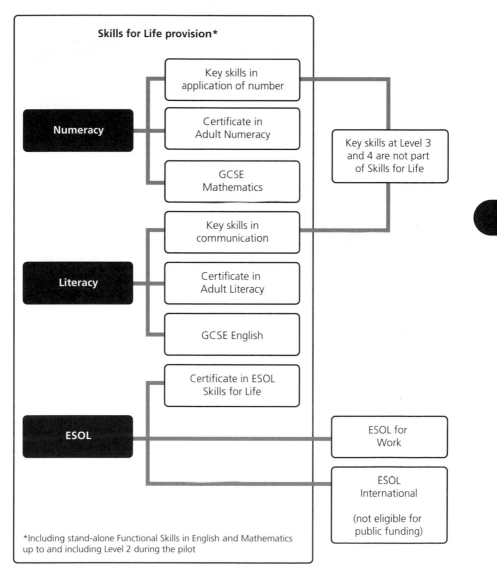

Skills for Life provision*

Key skills in application of number

Certificate in Adult Numeracy

Numeracy

GCSE Mathematics

Key skills at Level 3 and 4 are not part of Skills for Life

Key skills in communication

Certificate in Adult Literacy

Literacy

GCSE English

Certificate in ESOL Skills for Life

ESOL

ESOL for Work

ESOL International

(not eligible for public funding)

*Including stand-alone Functional Skills in English and Mathematics up to and including Level 2 during the pilot

Adult Numeracy and Literacy

There are a number of numeracy and literacy qualifications that fall under the umbrella term Skills for Life, including key skills and GCSEs in English and mathematics. In the adult sector, there are two qualifications available at five levels, the Certificate in Adult Numeracy and Certificate in Adult Literacy.

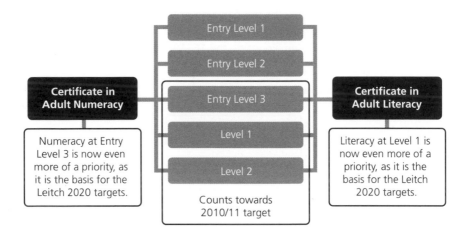

The level at which the learner achieves the qualification determines whether it contributes to the government target. There are a number of funding traits that are shared by all these certificates:

- learners are automatically eligible for fee remission (fully funded);
- they carry a basic skills programme weighting of 1.4 (F) in the adult learner-responsive funding model and 1.5 (C) in the employer-responsive funding model;
- basic skills learners, as defined by the LSC, have a 1.12 disadvantage uplift in the adult learner-responsive funding model;
- the funding rates are unlisted in the adult learner-responsive funding model and listed in the employer-responsive funding model.

Unweighted and unlisted adult funding (2008/09)

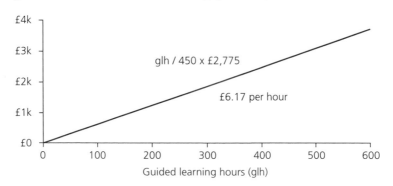

The funding rates for Certificates in Adult Numeracy and Literacy qualifications within the employer-responsive funding model are listed at 0.18 SLN. (*See Train to Gain section on page 96.*)

Supplementary information about literacy and numeracy and basic skills provision (including ESOL):

- GCSEs in English and mathematics at grades D–G contribute to Skills for Life targets at Level 1, and at grades A*–C at Level 2. However, they are not classed as basic skills qualifications, so neither attracts a programme weighting of 1.4, nor automatic fee remission.
- A two-year pilot of new functional skills qualifications started in September 2007, and it is anticipated they will replace the main key skills qualifications and Certificates in Adult Literacy and Numeracy from 2010/11 (*see page 60*).
- Providers can claim funding for 'non-approved' basic skills provision that is not on the National Qualifications Framework, such as at pre-Entry Level. However, non-approved Level 1 and 2 basic skills provision is discouraged and will no longer be part of the Skills for Life offer. As such it will attract neither a programme weighting of 1.4, nor automatic fee remission for basic skills enrolments.
- The *LSC Grant Letter 2008–09*, DIUS (November 2007) states that the volume of Skills for Life learners between 2008/09 and 2010/11 is planned to decrease by 2% in the adult learner-responsive funding model and increase by 6% in the employer-responsive funding model. Overall, the number of learners will remain constant at 1,227,000 for the next three years. Therefore, to achieve the ambitious Skills for Life targets the expectation is that providers will reduce non-approved, and low-level approved, non-target bearing Skills for Life in favour of target-bearing Skills for Life (particularly numeracy, for which there is a national marketing campaign).
- From 2006/07 the LSC stopped funding short, three- and six-hour Skills for Life diagnostics and taster sessions via further education funding.
- Learners on a numeracy or literacy basic skills enrolment should not be charged tuition fees, nor fees for any other aspect directly relating to their enrolment. Additional non-basic skills enrolments would not be eligible for remission funding and the learner would normally pay a fee (unless the learner is otherwise eligible for fee remission). The LSC no longer funds candidates to take stand-alone Skills for Life tests, but providers can charge a fee for this service.
- Learners on a numeracy or literacy course are not eligible for Additional Learning Support (ALS) funding if the intention is to use it to further support their numeracy and literacy skills.

English for Speakers of Other Languages

LSC funded courses in English for Speakers of Other Languages (ESOL) fall under the umbrella term Skills for Life and are for learners who require language skills to perform the necessities of daily life. ESOL, unlike English as a Foreign Language (EFL), is supported by the Government in an effort to help people settle into the UK.

The main ESOL qualification is the Certificate in ESOL Skills for Life, which is available at five levels and contains three mandatory units at each level.

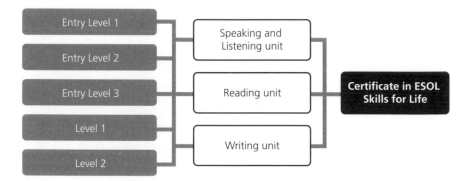

Individual units can be funded and enrolled on separately, but until the learner achieves the full certificate they cannot contribute to the Government's Skills for Life targets (Entry Level 3 and above for the original target and Level 1 for the new Leitch target). Learners that achieve the various units at different levels are known as having a 'spiky profile'. Once all three units have been achieved, the full certificate is awarded at the lowest level.

Certificate in ESOL Skills for Life: 'spiky profile' example

The basic skills programme weighting of 1.4 and disadvantage uplift of 1.12 are funded in the same way as for the Certificate in Adult Numeracy and Literacy. However, in 2007/08 automatic fee remission for ESOL enrolments was removed. This means that unless learners are eligible for fee remission (such as being on income-related benefits) a fee element is deducted from the funding (*see fee element section on page 46*).

Funding rates for ESOL Skills for Life units and qualifications within the adult learner-responsive funding models are unlisted. This means the funding rate is based on the actual number of glh (as described in the formula chapter). The graph below shows that the unweighted funding per glh is: £6.17 for the fully funded learner and £3.55 for the fee-paying co-funded learner. Therefore £2.62 has been deducted for the fee element.

Adult learner-responsive ESOL Skills for Life funding (unweighted)

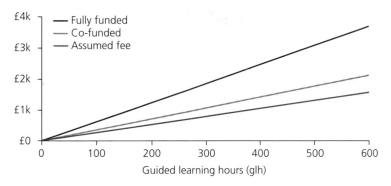

The funding rates for ESOL qualifications within the employer-responsive funding model are listed at 0.18 SLN (*see Train to Gain section on page 96*).

Certificate in ESOL for Work

Following the Government's review of ESOL provision in 2006, a new suite of ESOL for Work (EfW) qualifications were introduced in August 2007. These qualifications have been developed to 'support a shorter, more job-focused, practical approach to English language skills'. EfW qualifications are not part of Skills for Life and therefore do not contribute to government targets, nor do they attract a programme weighting of 1.4 or disadvantage uplift of 1.12 within the learner-responsive funding formula. The LSC has listed the EfW qualification rate at 150 SLN glh; given that most learners will be in work, they will generate the lower co-funding.

ESOL for Work	SLN glh	SLN	Co-funding (unweighted)
Entry 3 & Level 1	150	0.333r	£532

Certificate in ESOL International

These new international ESOL qualifications are different from EfW, as they are 'intended primarily for the overseas market and for those who want or need an internationally recognised qualification'. They are not eligible for LSC funding, nor do they contribute to government targets. They will include the International English Language Testing System (IELTS) from 2008/09.

Key skills and entitlement

Key skills funding

Key skills qualifications are primarily designed to be part of a full-time 16–18 learner programme and are mandatory in the Apprenticeship Framework. There six key skills qualifications (three standard and three 'wider' key skills), and all are available from Level 1 through to Level 4.

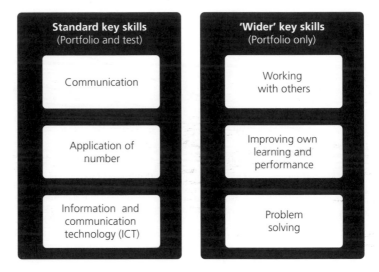

The standard key skills funding rate across all funding models and at all levels is listed at 36 SLN glh, while 'wider' key skills in the learner- responsive models (with the exception of school sixth forms), are unlisted.

Key skills	SLN glh	SLN	Unweighted funding at £2860 16–18 rate
Standard	36	0.08	£229
Wider	unlisted	glh / 450	SLN x £2860

Three new qualifications are being piloted to replace the three standard key skills. Known as functional skills, the English, mathematics and ICT qualifications will be unlisted during the pilot for colleges, and listed at 36 SLN glh for schools.

> **Note**
>
> Key skills in application of number and communication at Level 1 and Level 2 contribute to the Government's numeracy and literacy Public Service Agreement (PSA) target. In line with other basic-skills qualifications, they have a programme weighting of 1.4 (F).

Entitlement funding

Funding for 16–18 entitlement was introduced from 2000/01 to support a new approach to 16–18 education ('Curriculum 2000'). The Government introduced new qualifications (e.g. AS-levels) and provided funding to ensure that all 16–18-year-old learners acquired skills in literacy, numeracy and IT. The entitlement funding in 2008/09 pays for the regular tutorials and enrichment activities that are delivered in addition to the main programme and key skills. Learners eligible for entitlement funding must be aged under 19 on 31 August in the calendar year in which they start their programme of study, be studying on a full-time basis as defined by the LSC, and are expected to be enrolled on at least one key skill qualification.

Therefore, entitlement funding is found in the 16–18 funding model, alongside the main qualifications and key skills.

Entitlement funding	SLN glh	SLN	Unweighted funding at £2945 school sixth-form rate
Tutorial and enrichment per year	114	0.253r	£746

Key skills and entitlement

There have been two significant changes concerning the funding of key skills with entitlement. Firstly, from 2008/09 they will both be included within the 1.75 SLN per learner per year cap. Secondly, the previous funding methodology assumed one key skill would be delivered each year, which was funded within the entitlement element. The methodology for 2008/09 has changed because entitlement funding no longer includes funding for key skills, which as shown below, are funded individually.

Example programme with key skills and entitlement	SLN glh	SLN	Unweighted funding
BTEC Introductory Diploma	450	1	£2945
Key skills in communication	36	0.08	£236
Entitlement	114	0.253	£746
Total learner funding	**600**	**1.333**	**£3927**

These changes will alter the amount of funding generated by some 16–18 full-time providers significantly. For example, if a provider claimed entitlement funding without delivering key skills, all other factors held constant, their funding will reduce by more than £200 per learner. Conversely, a provider delivering two key skills will generate more funding.

Academic provision

This chapter focuses on the funding for the majority of the academic and applied curriculum at Levels 2 and 3. The qualifications are delivered to 16–18-year-olds within school sixth forms as well as 16–18-year-olds and adults within colleges. Therefore, this chapter lists all three types of unweighted funding within the 16–18 and adult learner-responsive funding models (school sixth forms, 16–18 college and 19+). Where appropriate, the deduction made for the adult fee element is also listed. As outlined in the formula chapter, unweighted funding is calculated by multiplying the listed Standard Learner Numbers (SLNs) by these national funding rates.

school sixth forms	£2945
16–18 college	£2860
19+ fully funded	£2775
19+ co-funded	£2775 x 42.5%

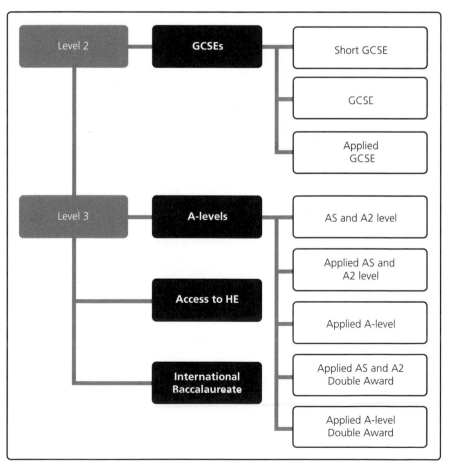

The GCSE curriculum

General Certificates of Secondary Education (GCSEs) were first introduced in 1986 to replace O-levels and Certificates of Secondary Education. In 1996 the Short GCSE was introduced (half the size and funding) and in 2002 the Applied GCSE was introduced (double the size and funding). In 2005/06 school sixth forms and colleges claimed approximately £0.6m for Short GCSEs, £110m for GCSEs and £6 m for Applied GCSEs.

Although GCSEs are generally studied at school in Years 10 and 11 (14- and 15-year-olds) they are also popular within post-16 education, particularly as part of a progression pathway to Level 3 and university. Part-time adults also study GCSEs during the evening, which usually requires fewer teaching hours. Therefore, the LSC has two listed funding rates for each GCSE, with an evening rate 40% lower than the day rate.

GCSE listed rates and funding when studied during the *day*

GCSE SLNs (day)	SLN glh		SLN
Short GCSE	50		0.111
GCSE	100		0.222
Applied GCSE	200		0.444
GCSE funding (day)	Unweighted funding		
	School	16–18 college	19+
Short GCSE	£327	£318	£308
GCSE	£654	£636	£617
Applied GCSE	£1309	£1271	£1233

GCSE listed rates and funding when studied during the *evening*

GCSE SLNs (evening)	SLN glh	SLN
Short GCSE	30	0.067
GCSE	60	0.133
Applied GCSE	120	0.267
GCSE funding (evening)	Unweighted funding	
	16–18 college	19+
Short GCSE	£191	£185
GCSE	£381	£370
Applied GCSE	£763	£740

The table below is an example of how funding might be claimed for a GCSE programme at a school sixth form:

Example GCSE programme	SLN	Unweighted funding for a school
10 GCSEs	1.111	£3272
Entitlement	0.253	£746
Total SLN and funding	1.364	£4018

Providers cannot claim full funding for adults studying GCSEs unless they meet one of the fee remission eligibility criteria (such as being on income-related benefits). The table below lists the amount of funding that would be deducted if the adult learner is expected to pay fees (co-funded).

GCSE adult fee deduction	LSC deduction for fee element	
	Day	Evening
Short GCSE	£131	£79
GCSE	£262	£157
Applied GCSE	£524	£315

Supplementary information about GCSEs

- GCSEs have a two-tier structure in terms of levels of attainment, with grades D–G equivalent to Level 1 (foundation) and grades A*–C equivalent to Level 2 (higher).
- GCSEs have the 'potential to contribute' to the Government's full Level 2 Public Service Agreement (PSA) target (see page 13). This is because the current definition of a full Level 2 is 'equivalent to 5 GCSEs at grades A*–C'. Therefore, every GCSE is allocated 20% of a full Level 2 within the Learning Aim Database and consequently categorised by the LSC as a priority qualification.
- GCSEs in English and mathematics contribute to the Government's Skills for Life PSA target. Yet, unlike most other numeracy and literacy qualifications, they are eligible for neither the fee remission nor the basic skills programme weighting and disadvantage uplift.
- GCSEs in English and mathematics grade A*–C are 'proxy qualifications' for key skills in application of number and communication. This means the learner is exempt from the relevant key skill test. GCSE Computing, GCSE Information Systems and GCSE ICT qualifications are proxy qualifications for key skills in ICT.

The A-level curriculum

The General Certificate in Education (GCE) at Advanced Level (A-level) was introduced in 1951. In 2000 the Government introduced Curriculum 2000, which split the six-unit A-level into a three-unit AS (Advanced Subsidiary) and three-unit A2 examination. In 2005 A-levels in applied subjects were introduced to replace the Advanced Vocational Certificate of Education (AVCE), and in 2008 a new A* grade is being introduced for A2 level exam results above 90%. A-levels are traditionally studied by 16–18-year-olds in school sixth forms, sixth-form colleges and further-education colleges after completing GCSEs. They are also studied in the evening by about 50,000 adults, which usually requires fewer teaching hours.

A-level funding rates are complicated by three factors. Firstly, the listed rate for AS and A2 General Studies, which on average is only taught one hour per week, is 76% lower than for other AS and A2 qualifications. The LSC also considered reducing the rate for AS and A2 Critical Thinking and will consider it again for 2009/10. Secondly, as with GCSEs, the evening rate is 60% lower than the day-rate (with the exception of AS and A2 General Studies). Finally, unlike GCSEs, the Applied AS and A2 qualifications are not simply double the A-level rate.

A-level listed rates and funding when studied during the *day*:

A-level SLNs (day)	SLN glh	SLN
AS or A2 excl. General Studies	150	0.333
AS or A2 General Studies	36	0.08
Applied AS or A2	180	0.4
Applied A-level	360	0.8
Applied AS or A2 Double Award	450	1
Applied A-level Double Award	900	2
A-level funding (day)	**Unweighted funding (national rate)**		
	School sixth form	16–18 college	19+
AS or A2 excl. General Studies	£982	£953	£925
AS or A2 General Studies	£236	£229	£222
Applied AS or A2	£1178	£1144	£1110
Applied A-level	£2356	£2288	£2220
Applied AS or A2 Double Award	£2945	£2860	£2775
Applied A-level Double Award	£5890	£5720	£5550

A-level listed rates and funding when studied during the *evening*

A-level SLNs (evening)	SLN glh	SLN
AS or A2 excl. General Studies	90	0.2
AS or A2 General Studies	36	0.08
Applied AS or A2	108	0.24
Applied A-level	216	0.48
Applied AS or A2 Double Award	270	0.6
Applied A-level Double Award	540	1.2
A-level funding (evening)	Unweighted funding (national rate)	
	16–18 college	19+
AS or A2 excl. General Studies	£572	£555
AS or A2 General Studies	£229	£222
Applied AS or A2	£686	£666
Applied A-level	£1373	£1332
Applied AS or A2 Double Award	£1716	£1665
Applied A-level Double Award	£3432	£3330

The table below is an example of how funding might be claimed for a first- year A-level programme at a school sixth form.

Example A-level programme	SLN	Unweighted funding for a school
4 AS non-General Studies	1.333	£3927
AS General Studies	0.08	£236
Key skills in communication	0.08	£236
Entitlement	0.253	£746
Total SLN and funding	**1.747**	**£5144**

In terms of adult fees, 42.5% of the unweighted funding would be deducted if the learner were ineligible for remission. In the case of an AS or A2, this would mean that £393 would be deducted. However, a first full Level 3 adult learner under the age of 25 would be eligible for remission via the Level 3 entitlement. This is because any combination of four AS or A2 levels is equivalent to a full Level 3 qualification (25% each). This also means that A-levels are a high funding priority, as they have the potential to contribute to the full Level 3 Public Service Agreement (PSA) target (*see page 13*).

Access to HE Diploma

Access to HE qualifications were established in the 1970s, and in 2008/09 all learners will be enrolled on the newly validated Access to HE Diploma. These courses are specially designed to prepare adult learners for entry into higher education by providing the underpinning knowledge and skills needed to progress to a degree or diploma course. As such, they are Level 3 qualifications, which generally provide adults with a one-year alternative to the traditional two-year A-level pathway.

Access to HE Diplomas are available at most further education colleges, in a wide range of subjects. Approximately 20,000 Access to HE learners apply to universities each year. One of the interesting features of these qualifications is that they are neither part of the National Qualifications Framework (NQF), nor regulated by the Qualifications and Curriculum Authority (QCA). The approval of Access to HE courses is managed by the universities' own quality assurance organisation, the Quality Assurance Agency for Higher Education (QAA).

Funding rates for Access to HE qualifications within the adult learner-responsive funding model are the same as the rates for National Vocational Qualifications (NVQs). There is a listed rate for enrolments of 450 glh and above (full-time) and an unlisted rate for enrolments below 450 glh (part-time). For both the Access to HE and NVQ this represents a change for 2008/09, as in previous years part-time enrolments had a listed rate.

Access to HE	SLN glh	SLN	Unweighted funding
450 glh or more	520	1.156	£3207
Less than 450 glh	Provider glh	glh / 450	SLN x £2775

68

If the learner were ineligible for fee remission, 42.5% of the unweighted funding would be deducted as the fee element (*see fee element section on page 46*).

Access to HE fee deduction	Full-time	Part-time
Access to HE	£1363	SLN x £2775 x 42.5%

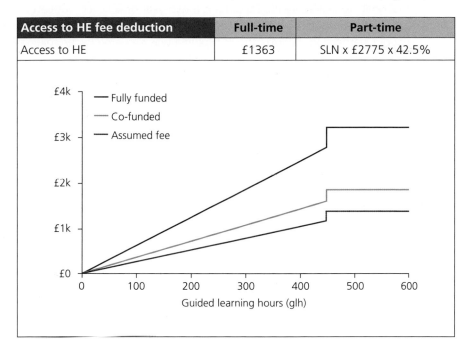

Supplementary information about Access to HE

- Access to HE courses are classified as full Level 3 courses, even though they are neither on the National Qualifications Framework (NQF) nor above the 595 glh threshold (excluding NVQs) for a full Level 3 qualification. This means that a first Full Level 3 learner who achieves the qualification would contribute to the Department for Innovation, Universities and Skills (DIUS) Public Service Agreement (PSA) target at Level 3. It is also specifically designed to progress learners into HE, and participation in HE is a PSA target for the Department for Children, Schools and Families (DCSF) (*see page 13*).
- As a contributor to PSA targets in two government departments, Access to HE is a high-priority qualification. This is of course maintained only when a sufficient percentage of learners are achieving the qualification, and preferably progressing into higher education.
- As a full Level 3 qualification, first full Level 3 learners under the age of 25 would be eligible for fee remission via the Level 3 entitlement. Some adults enrolled on an Access to HE Diploma would be first full Level 2 learners, in which case, as 'jumpers', they would be eligible to remission at any age via the Level 2 entitlement.
- LSC funding for Access to HE in 2006/07 was approximately £68m.

International Baccalaureate

The International Baccalaureate (IB) Diploma is a two-year qualification at Level 3 designed to lead to progression to university, and is studied predominantly by 16–19-year-old learners. In 2006/07 the IB Diploma was delivered by 17 colleges and 25 school sixth forms across 32 local authorities.

The IB Diploma qualification consists of six certificates and learners usually study three at a higher level (240 glh) and three at standard level (150 glh):
1. own language
2. second language
3. individuals and society (e.g. history)
4. the arts
5. experimental sciences
6. mathematics and computer science

There are also three compulsory core requirements:
1. extended essay (4000 words)
2. theory of knowledge
3. creativity, action, service

The certificates are scored out of 7 and each core element is worth one point (with up to a further additional three points depending on grades). A minimum of 24 points are required to be awarded the IB Diploma. UCAS points range from 280 for 24 points (equivalent to 3.5 C-graded A-levels) to 768 for 45 points (equivalent to 6.4 A-graded A-levels).

The full IB Diploma is credited as offering a broader mix of subjects than most A-level programmes. As such, it is funded as a large single programme, and the table below shows how the elements might be delivered alongside standard 16–18 tutorial and enrichment activities.

Example IB Diploma	Guided learning hours over two years
Three higher-level certificates	720
Three standard-level certificates	450
Extended essay	n/a
Theory of knowledge	128
Creativity, action, service	128
Tutorials and other enrichment activities	152
Total guided learning hours	1578

When setting the listed funding rate for the IB Diploma, the LSC has had to take account of the 114 SLN glh per year entitlement for the 16–18-year-old tutorial and enrichment activities. Therefore, it has deducted 228 glh from the 1578 glh and listed the IB Diploma rate at 1350 glh.

IB Diploma SLN	1350 SLN glh	3 SLN

The funding, excluding inflation, for 2009/10, would be:

IB Diploma (two years)	Unweighted funding (national rate)		
	School	16–18	19+
	£8835	£8580	£8325

Once entitlement is included, the funding increases as follows:

IB Diploma plus entitlement (two years)	SLN	Unweighted funding for school sixth form
International Baccalaureate	3	£8835
Entitlement	0.507	£1492
Total SLN and funding	3.507	£10,327*

Therefore, funding in 2008/09 would be approximately half the total:

IB Diploma plus entitlement (year 1)	SLN	Unweighted funding for 16–18 college
International Baccalaureate per year	1.5	£4418
Entitlement per year	0.253	£746
Total SLN and funding	1.753	£5164*

* The LSC has attempted to list the SLNs that would generate maximum funding. However, the 3.507 total SLN very slightly exceeds the learner SLN cap of 3.5 (1.75 per year). Therefore, the unweighted funding for a school sixth form would actually be £10,308 over two years (excluding inflation). Also, SLN Values are allocated to each academic year based on the percentage of calendar days (between enrolment start and end date) in the given year. Therefore, to prevent one of the years further exceeding the 1.75 SLN cap, the number of calendar days in the first year would need to be identical to the number of days in the second year.

BTEC provision

In 1996 the Business and Technology Education Council (BTEC), the country's leading provider of vocational qualifications, merged with the University of London Examinations & Assessment Council (ULEAC), one of the major exam boards for GCSEs and A-levels, to become Edexcel. BTECs are unit- and portfolio-based work-related qualifications that have been around since 1984. In 2007 more than a million young people and adults were enrolled on a BTEC course.

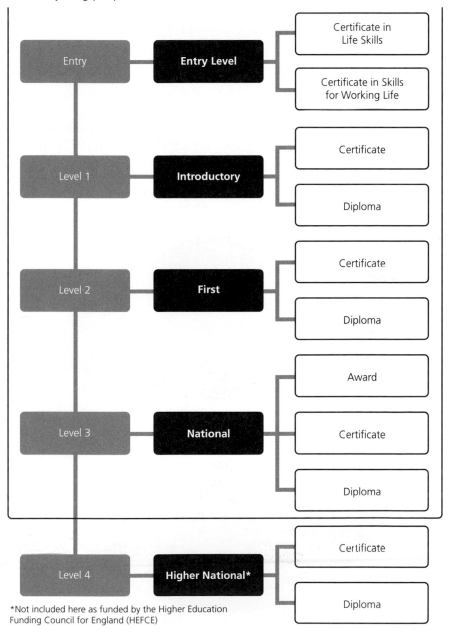

*Not included here as funded by the Higher Education
Funding Council for England (HEFCE)

BTEC Entry and Introductory qualifications

BTEC Entry

BTEC Entry Certificates in Skills for Working Life and Life Skills either develop the initial skills for a broad work sector or build confidence for everyday life. They are particularly popular among learners with learning difficulties or those who struggle with traditional learning. The funding rates are unlisted for these qualifications, so a 36-hour course for a 16-year-old in college would generate an unweighted funding of (36 / 450) x £2860 = £229.

BTEC Introductory

BTEC Introductory qualifications are at Level 1. They offer an entry point into an industry sector and encourage the development of personal and work-related skills. The qualification model is composed of two qualifications, the four-unit Certificate and the eight-unit Diploma. The Introductory Certificate is 'nested' within the Introductory Diploma, which means the Certificate units are a sub-set of the Diploma. Providers can therefore deliver the Certificate and then 'top up' to the Diploma by offering the additional four units required for the Diploma.

Edexcel recommends 180 glh for the Introductory Certificate and 360 glh for the Introductory Diploma, but the LSC analysed actual provider durations and has listed the BTEC Introductory funding rates as follows:

BTEC Introductory (Level 1) School sixth forms	SLN glh	SLN	Unweighted funding
BTEC Introductory Certificate	225	0.5	£1473
BTEC Introductory Diploma	450	1	£2945

In most cases, the SLN glh for the school sixth forms is the same as for colleges. However, the LSC can set unlisted rates for colleges, which they have chosen to do for the Introductory Certificate.

BTEC Introductory (Level 1) Colleges	SLN glh	SLN	Unweighted funding*
BTEC Introductory Certificate	Unlisted	glh / 450	SLN x £2860
BTEC Introductory Diploma	450	1	£2860

*Less 3% for adult fully funded learners

The table below contains the unweighted funding for a potential BTEC Introductory Diploma programme at a school sixth form.

Example BTEC Introductory programme for school sixth forms	SLN glh	SLN	Unweighted funding
BTEC Introductory Diploma	450	1	£2945
Key skills in communication	36	0.08	£236
Entitlement	114	0.253	£746
Total learner funding	600	1.333	£3927

BTEC First Certificate and Diploma

BTEC Firsts are at Level 2 and are the vocational equivalent of GCSEs grades A*–C. Traditionally they are used primarily in the further education sector. In recent years they have also increasingly been delivered by schools. There are over 60 BTEC Firsts comprising two qualifications – the three-unit First Certificate and the six-unit First Diploma. The First Certificate is 'nested' within the First Diploma. Providers can therefore deliver the Certificate in the first instance, with provision to offer the additional three units required for the Diploma subsequently.

The BTEC Firsts at Level 2 are funded at the same rate and in the same way as the BTEC Introductory at Level 1. The rates for schools are listed:

BTEC Firsts (Level 2) School sixth forms	SLN glh	SLN	Unweighted funding
BTEC First Certificate	225	0.5	£1473
BTEC First Diploma	450	1	£2945

The First Diploma rate for colleges is the same as the school sixth forms rate, while the First Certificate rate is unlisted.

BTEC Firsts (Level 2) Colleges	SLN glh	SLN	Unweighted funding*
BTEC First Certificate	Provider glh	glh / 450	SLN x £2860
BTEC First Diploma	450	1	£2860

*Less 3% for adult fully funded

The graph below shows the listed and unlisted approach to unweighted funding for the BTEC Firsts in colleges (assuming a maximum glh range of 100 to 300 for the Certificate and 300 to 500 for the Diploma).

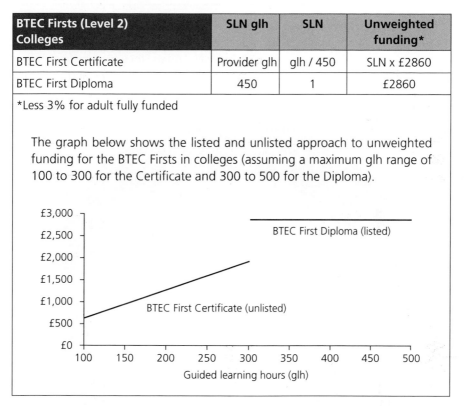

> ### Note
> To prevent providers from claiming too much funding, the LSC has created 'conversion' learning aims for progressions from a First Certificate to a Diploma.

Supplementary information about BTEC Firsts
- BTEC First Diplomas exceed the 325 glh threshold (excluding NVQs) for a full Level 2 qualification. Therefore, first full Level 2 learners that achieve the Diploma will contribute to the Government's full Level 2 Public Service Agreement (PSA) target. In funding terms this places the First Diploma into the high priority classification.
- Adult first full Level 2 learners enrolled on the First Diploma would be fee remitted as part of the Level 2 Entitlement. The First Diploma is also eligible for funding under the Train to Gain scheme (see page 96).
- Some BTEC Firsts are technical certificates within Apprenticeship frameworks. For example, the BTEC First Diploma in Engineering is one of the options within the Level 2 Engineering Apprenticeship.

BTEC National Award, Certificate and Diploma

The Level 3 BTEC Nationals have for nearly 25 years been the vocational equivalent of A-levels in colleges, and in recent years have also increasingly been delivered by school sixth forms. There are over 250 BTEC Nationals; they are portfolio based and as 'nested' qualifications they consist of Awards, Certificates and Diplomas within a single framework.

In terms of funding the BTEC Nationals, the LSC considered average provider delivery patterns, and for 2008/09 has kept the rates for the six-unit Award and 12-unit Certificate above the awarding body recommended guided learning hours (glh). However, for 2008/09 they have reduced the 18-unit Diploma rate from the equivalent of 1440 glh down to the awarding body recommended 1080 glh.

BTEC National (Level 3)	SLN glh	SLN	Unweighted funding (16–18 college)
BTEC National Award	450	1	£2860
BTEC National Certificate	900	2	£5720
BTEC National Diploma	1080	2.4	£6864

As these are 'nested' qualifications, learners achieving the BTEC National Award can study the additional units to achieve the Certificate or Diploma. The LSC has created learning-aim 'conversion codes' in order to fund this.

BTEC Nationals (Level 3)	SLN glh	SLN	Unweighted funding (16–18)
Conversion from BTEC Award to BTEC Diploma	630	1.4	£4004
Conversion from BTEC Award to BTEC Certificate	450	1	£2860
Conversion from BTEC Certificate to BTEC Diploma	180	0.4	£1144

The 16–18-year-old funding for a two-year BTEC National Diploma is likely to include key skills and entitlement for tutorials and enrichment activities. Therefore, funding would be as follows (excluding 2009/10 inflation).

BTEC National Programme	SLN glh	SLN	Unweighted funding (16–18)*
BTEC National Diploma	1080	2.400	£6864
One key skill over two years	228	0.507	£1449
Entitlement (two years)	36	0.080	£229
Total learner (over two years)	**1344**	**2.987**	**£8542**

* Increase by 3% for school sixth forms, and reduce by 3% for fully funded adults.

BTEC National Certificates and Diplomas are full Level 3 qualifications, as they exceed the current 595 glh threshold (excluding NVQs) for fullness at Level 3. Therefore, first full Level 3 learners that achieve their full qualification would count towards the Government's Public Service Agreement (PSA) target. First full Level 3 adult learners under the age of 25 would also be eligible for fee remission via the Level 3 Entitlement.

The BTEC Foundation Diploma in Art and Design is also at Level 3, and in 2007/08 grew to nine units and became a full Level 3. The awarding body glh is 600, although it will be funded in 2008/09 at 645 SLN glh (1.433 SLN). This generates unweighted 16–18 college funding of £4099.

Note

The 18-unit BTEC National Diploma is funded at the same rate as the 18-unit OCR Level 3 National Extended Diploma. The 12-unit BTEC National Certificate is funded at the same rate as the 12-unit OCR Level 3 National Diploma. Finally, the six-unit BTEC National Award is funded at the same rate as the six-unit OCR Level 3 National Certificate.

Diploma provision

As part of the ongoing 14–19 qualification reform programme, the Department for Children, Schools and Families (DCSF), the Qualifications and Curriculum Authority (QCA), the Skills for Business Network (SfBN) and awarding bodies such as Edexcel have developed the new Diploma qualification. The QCA describes the Diploma as being 'about learning a range of widely applicable skills and knowledge, set within a 'specialised context – a specified group of sectors and subjects'.

The Diploma programmes are available at Levels 1, 2 and 3.

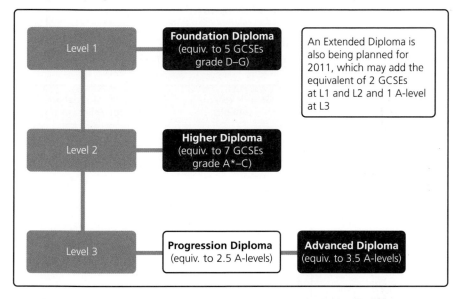

The main subjects are known as lines of learning. From September 2008 the first five come on stream. There will be 14 vocational lines of learning available in 2010 and a further three academic ones from 2011. The Diploma has a common structure across all 17 lines of learning. Providers need to be separately approved to deliver each line of learning, and there is a strong emphasis on taking account of the partnership environment within which the Diplomas are designed to be delivered.

Diploma lines available in 2008/09	Programme weighting within provider factor*	
	Level 1	Levels 2 & 3
Construction and the built environment	1.3 (C)	1.3 (C)
Creative and media	1.3 (C)	1.3 (C)
Engineering	1.3 (C)	1.3 (C)
Information technology	1.12 (B)	1.3 (C)
Society, health and development	1.12 (B)	1.12 (B)

*Applied only to the principal learning and project elements of the Diploma

Foundation Diploma

The Foundation Diploma is at Level 1 and requires 600 glh. In terms of average length of study, it is equivalent to five GCSEs and would normally be studied in one year if the learner was in post-compulsory education, or two years if taken at the same time as the key stage 4 national curriculum programme of study.

Diplomas at all levels balance practical and theoretical understanding within three components, as outlined in the diagram below:

Foundation Diploma: 600 glh
Source: *The Diploma: an overview of the qualification,* Version 3, QCA (2008)

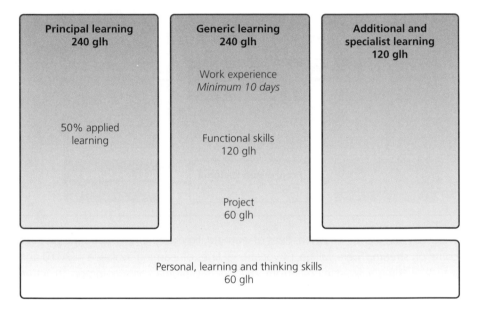

The diploma catalogues contain all the principal learning and project qualifications that are available to learners at each level, as well as a full listing of the functional skills and additional specialist learning options relevant to a specific line of learning. The diploma catalogues can be accessed on the online National Database of Accredited Qualifications (NDAQ) at www.accreditedqualifications.org.uk

Each component part of the diploma has a Standard Learner Number (SLN) Value and funding is calculated separately for each component. Therefore, learners would need to enrol on each element, although an overarching programme code within the Individualised Learner Record (ILR) would link the elements together and determine whether the learner had passed or failed the diploma. Functional skills, the project, and the additional and specialist learning elements are also available for accreditation as separate learning aims in their own right.

The funding rates for the Foundation Diploma include 30 SLN glh for the 'costs of collaboration'. Full-time 16–18-year-olds are also eligible for entitlement funding of 114 SLN glh (enrichment and tutorial activities). In the example below, the learner is enrolled on all three functional skills elements.

Foundation Diploma (Level 1)	SLN glh	SLN
Principal learning	240	0.533
Project	60	0.133
Functional skills – English	36	0.080
Functional skills – ICT	36	0.080
Functional skills – mathematics	36	0.080
Additional and specialist learning	120	0.267
Personal learning and thinking skills	60	0.133
Costs of collaboration	30	0.067
Total (excl. entitlement)	618	1.373
16–18 entitlement	114	0.253
Total (incl. entitlement)	732	1.627

Foundation Diploma (Level 1)	Unweighted funding	
	School	16–18 college*
Principal learning	£1571	£1525
Project	£393	£381
Functional skills – English	£236	£229
Functional Skills – ICT	£236	£229
Functional Skills – mathematics	£236	£229
Additional and specialist learning	£785	£763
Personal learning and thinking skills	£393	£381
Costs of collaboration	£196	£191
Total (excl. entitlement)	£4044	£3928
16–18 entitlement	£746	£725
Total (incl. entitlement)	£4791	£4652

* Less 3% for fully funded adults

Higher Diploma

The Higher Diploma is at Level 2, and requires 800 glh. In terms of average length of study, it is equivalent to seven GCSEs and would normally be studied in one or two years if the learner is in post-compulsory education, or two years if taken at the same time as the key stage 4 national curriculum programme of study.

Higher Diploma: 800 glh

Source: *The Diploma: an overview of the qualification*, Version 3, QCA (2008)

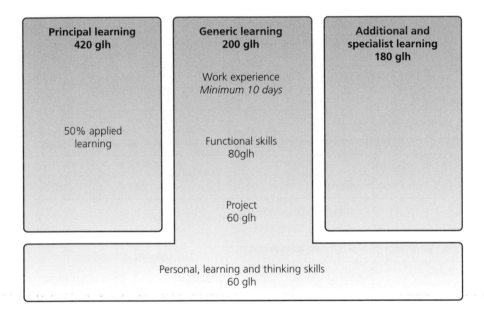

Principal learning 420 glh	Generic learning 200 glh	Additional and specialist learning 180 glh
	Work experience *Minimum 10 days*	
50% applied learning	Functional skills 80glh	
	Project 60 glh	

Personal, learning and thinking skills
60 glh

The funding rates include 40 SLN glh for the costs of collaboration. In the example below, the learner has already attained functional skills in ICT.

Higher Diploma (Level 2)	SLN glh	SLN
Principal learning	420	0.933
Project	60	0.133
Functional skills – English	36	0.080
Functional skills – mathematics	36	0.080
Additional and specialist learning	180	0.400
Personal learning and thinking skills	60	0.133
Costs of collaboration	40	0.089
Total	832	1.849

Higher Diploma (Level 2)	Unweighted funding	
	School	16–18 college*
Principal learning	£2749	£2669
Project	£393	£381
Functional skills – English	£236	£229
Functional Skills – mathematics	£236	£229
Additional and specialist learning	£1178	£1144
Personal learning and thinking skills	£393	£381
Costs of collaboration	£262	£254
Total (excl. entitlement)	£5445	£5288

* Less 3% for fully funded adults

As previously mentioned, a 16–18-year-old can study a Level 2 Higher Diploma over one year. The problem with this is that the 1.849 SLN exceeds the 1.75 SLN annual cap. Therefore, if it were taught in one year, funding would be reduced by 0.099 SLN (5%). In the example below, it is studied over two years and the learner is also funded for two years of entitlement (tutorial and enrichment) at 114 SLN glh per year.

Higher Diploma (Level 2)	Unweighted funding	
	School	16–18 college*
Principal learning	£2749	£2669
Project	£393	£381
Functional skills – English	£236	£229
Functional skills – mathematics	£236	£229
Additional and specialist learning	£1178	£1144
Personal learning and thinking skills	£393	£381
Costs of collaboration	£262	£254
Total (excl. entitlement)	£5445	£5288
16–18 entitlement (two years)	£1492	£1449
Total (incl. entitlement)	£6937	£6737

* Excludes inflation for 2009/10. Less 3% for fully-funded adults

Note

Selecting the most appropriate timetable and overall duration (one or two years) will be particularly important for Higher Diploma learners.

Advanced Diploma

The Advanced Diploma is at Level 3 and requires 1080 glh. It is the equivalent, in terms of the Universities and Colleges Admissions Service (UCAS) points, to three-and-a-half A-levels. It would normally be studied in post-compulsory education full time over two years.

Advanced Diploma: 1080 glh

Source: *The Diploma: an overview of the qualification*, Version 3, QCA (2008)

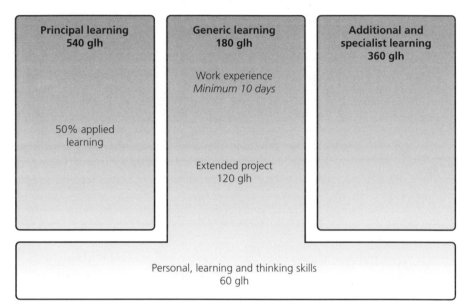

Principal learning 540 glh	Generic learning 180 glh	Additional and specialist learning 360 glh
	Work experience *Minimum 10 days*	
50% applied learning		
	Extended project 120 glh	

Personal, learning and thinking skills
60 glh

The funding rates include 54 SLN glh for the costs of collaboration, and for 16–18-year-olds may include entitlement funding.

Advanced Diploma (Level 3)	SLN glh	SLN
Principal learning	540	1.200
Extended project	120	0.267
Additional and specialist learning	360	0.800
Personal learning and thinking skills	60	0.133
Costs of collaboration	54	0.120
Total (excl. entitlement)	**1134**	**2.520**
16–18 entitlement (two years)	228	0.507
Total (incl. entitlement)	**1362**	**3.027**

Advanced Diploma (Level 3)	Unweighted funding	
	School	16–18 college*
Principal learning	£3534	£3432
Extended project	£785	£763
Additional and specialist learning	£2356	£2288
Personal learning and thinking skills	£393	£381
Costs of collaboration	£353	£343
Total (excl. entitlement)	**£7421**	**£7207**
16–18 entitlement (two years)	£1492	£1449
Total (incl. entitlement)	**£8914**	**£8656**

* Excludes inflation for 2009/10. Less 3% for fully funded adults

There is also a Progression Diploma at Level 3, which is a sub-set of the Advanced Diploma, and equivalent in terms of UCAS points to 2.5 A-levels.

Progression Diploma (Level 3)	SLN glh	SLN
Principal learning	540	1.200
Extended project	120	0.267
Personal learning and thinking skills	60	0.133
Costs of collaboration	36	0.080
Total	**756**	**1.680**

Advanced Diploma (Level 3)	Unweighted funding	
	School	16–18 college*
Principal learning	£3534	£3432
Extended project	£785	£763
Personal learning and thinking skills	£393	£381
Costs of collaboration	£236	£229
Total	**£4948**	**£4805**

*Less 3% for fully funded adults

Note

In March 2008 the DCSF announced an expansion of the diploma programme, with the introduction of extended diplomas from 2011/12. Available at Levels 1, 2 and 3, they will feature a further block of additional and/or specialist learning, and an 'extended core' of mathematics and English content. This is significant at Level 3, as it is expected to be the equivalent, in UCAS points, of 4.5 A-levels.

Occupational provision

This section is called Occupational provision because it contains: a programme that can be tailored to quickly progress 16–18-year-olds into employment, a qualification based on national occupational standards and two learning programmes designed to raise occupational skills.

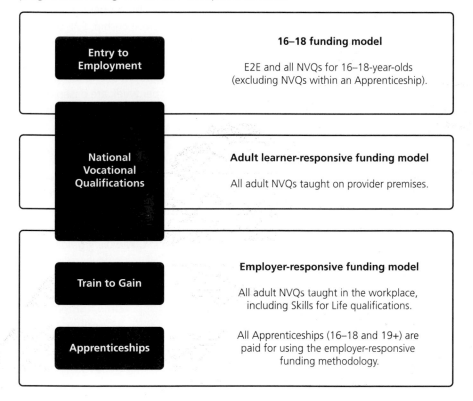

As the diagram above shows, National Vocational Qualifications (NVQs) can be funded from any one of the three funding models. This qualification is also particularly complex in terms of funding for 2008/09 because:

- There are 'higher' and 'lower' listed funding rates in the workplace, as well as different listed rates for Level 2 and Level 3.
- Previously FE funded workplace NVQs will be funded as Train to Gain.
- There is a listed and unlisted funding rate when the course is delivered on the provider's premises, as well as different programme weightings and fee elements between the employer-responsive and adult learner-responsive funding models.
- Stand-alone 16–18 NVQs in the workplace are not funded from the employer-responsive funding model, while 16–18 Apprenticeships are.
- They can be delivered as a stand-alone programme or within an Apprenticeship.
- Workplace NVQs often start mid-year and 'carry over' to the next year.

See page 92 for further information regarding the NVQ.

Entry to Employment

Entry to Employment (E2E) is a learning programme that has been available to 16–18-year-olds since 2003/04. E2E is designed to reduce the number of young people not in education, employment or training (NEET) by preparing them for progression to employment, further education or an Apprenticeship. E2E provides the opportunity for greater flexibility than more traditional 16–18-year-old programmes, as it is not time bound, specified in terms of guided learning hours, nor qualification driven (although qualifications will be appropriate and an incentive for some E2E learners). The duration, content and hours per week are based on the needs of each learner and funding will continue to be based on the number of weeks of learning attendance (as at midnight on the Monday of the week).

E2E funding has in the past been claimed by colleges and training providers as part of the work-based learning (WBL) contract. However, from 2008/09, E2E will be funded from within the new 16–18 funding model. This means that funding claims to the LSC will no longer be monthly, although many of the funding characteristics remain unchanged. These include a weekly rate and basic or enhanced bonuses if the learner achieves a qualification and progresses (see LSC eligibility guidance).

The 2008/09 E2E rates:

Entry to Employment	SLN	Unweighted funding
Weekly rate*	0.039	£112
Enhanced bonus (for achievement or positive progression)	0.063	£180
Basic bonus (for achievement or positive progression)	0.031	£89

*Entitlement funding cannot be added as it is included in the weekly rate.

Funding is therefore heavily dependent on the number of weeks a learner is on programme, rather than on a listed rate for a particular qualification type, or on the number of guided learning hours delivered.

Entry to Employment example	SLN	Unweighted funding (£2860 per SLN)
10 weeks on the BTEC Entry Level Certificate in Skills for Working Life	0.39	£1115
Enhanced progression bonus	0.063	£180
Basic achievement bonus	0.031	£89
Total	0.484	£1384

The use of Standard Learner Numbers (SLNs) and a national funding rate (NFR) applies to E2E. However, some elements in the provider factor (PF) for E2E do not apply in the same way as for other learners in the 16–18 funding model.

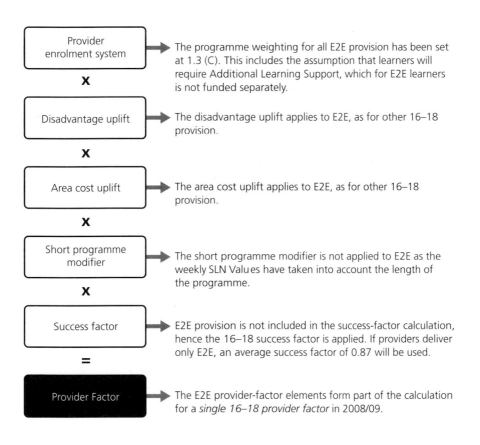

Hence the funding formula remains the same for E2E, with the exception of ALS, which is excluded as it is funded within the programme weighting:

SLN x NFR x PF = E2E funding

National Vocational Qualifications

National Vocational Qualifications (NVQs) are work-related, competence-based qualifications that are achieved through assessment and training.

NVQs are a mandatory component of the Apprenticeship Framework, but they can also be delivered on the provider's premises on a full-time basis, or for employers as part-time day or block release. Increasingly, they are also being delivered as stand-alone work-based qualifications on the employer's premises (usually as part of the Train to Gain programme). In funding terms, this makes the NVQ a relatively complex qualification, as they have listed and unlisted rates and can be funded from any one of the three new funding models:

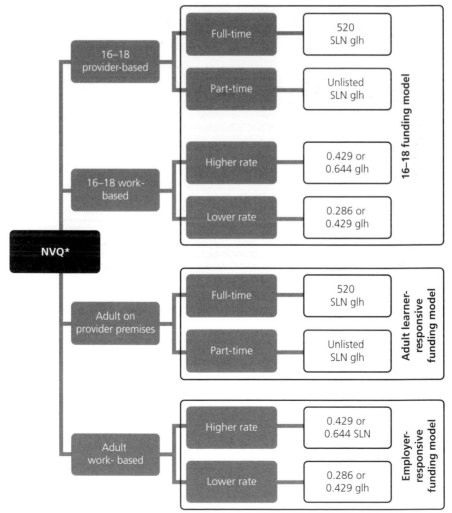

* Apprenticeships use the relevant lower NVQ rate

Higher and lower NVQ rates (in the workplace)

The work-based NVQs have two rates. The higher rate can only be claimed when the delivery includes underpinning knowledge and understanding or substantial skills development. The lower rate is always used when part of an Apprenticeship. (*See the Train to Gain section on page 96.*)

Full-time and part-time NVQ rates (on provider premises)

There are two rates within the adult learner-responsive funding models, for when 'all NVQ components are delivered at the provider's premises as part of a comprehensive programme of study'. The full-time rate can only be claimed for enrolments with planned guided learning hours (glh) of 450 or more per year.

16–18 NVQs rates with £2860 national funding rate:

NVQ workplace	SLN		Unweighted funding	
	Higher	Lower	Higher	Lower
NVQ 2	0.429	0.286	£1227	£818
NVQ 3	0.644	0.429	£1842	£1227
NVQ provider	**SLN**		**Unweighted funding**	
	Full-time	Part-time	Full-time	Part-time
NVQ (all levels)	1.156	unlisted	£3305	SLN x £2860

Adult NVQ unweighted funding with £2775 national funding rate:

NVQ workplace	Fee remitted		Non-fee remitted	
	Higher	Lower	Higher	Lower
NVQ 2	£1190	£794	£685	£456
NVQ 3	£1787	£1190	£1028	£685
NVQ provider	**Fee remitted**		**Non-fee remitted**	
	Full-time	Part-time	Full-time	Part-time
NVQ (all levels)	£3207	SLN x £2775	£3305	SLN x £2775 x 0.575

Note

All Level 2 and 3 NVQs are 'full', which means learners may contribute to the Government's PSA targets. Also, first full Level 2 adults are eligible for full funding, with the exception of Apprenticeships.

Apprenticeships

In 1994 Modern Apprenticeships were introduced to raise participation and extend the original programme beyond those employment sectors with no Apprenticeship tradition. Although the term 'modern' was dropped in 2004, by 2008 there were over 180 Apprenticeship frameworks on offer, with approximately 240,000 learners participating across England.

Apprenticeships are available at Level 2 (Apprenticeships) and Level 3 (Advanced Apprenticeships). Their frameworks are devised by the government-funded Sector Skills Councils (SSCs), which are employer-led bodies responsible for defining training requirements in their sector. Each apprenticeship Framework works to the same 'blueprint' (which is available online at www.Apprenticeships.org.uk).

Apprenticeship Framework 'blueprint':

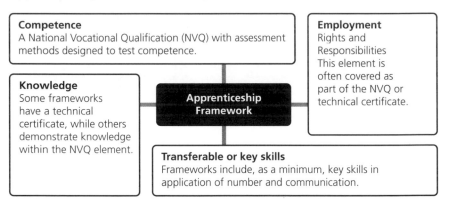

Competence
A National Vocational Qualification (NVQ) with assessment methods designed to test competence.

Knowledge
Some frameworks have a technical certificate, while others demonstrate knowledge within the NVQ element.

Apprenticeship Framework

Employment
Rights and Responsibilities
This element is often covered as part of the NVQ or technical certificate.

Transferable or key skills
Frameworks include, as a minimum, key skills in application of number and communication.

The LSC states that for employees aged 16–25, 'the Apprenticeship is the government's preferred option for vocational learners in this age group and they should be recruited onto the Apprenticeship programme wherever possible'. The table below contains an example framework:

Level 2 Retail Framework (112)	SLN	Unweighted 16–18 funding
Framework funding (funded with NVQ)	0.759	£2171
NVQ 2 in Retail Skills	0.286	£818
Level 2 Certificate in Retailing (incl. Employment Rights and Responsibilities)	0.3	£858
Key skills in communication	0.08	£229
Key skills in application of number	0.08	£229
Total framework funding	1.505	£4304

16–18-year-old and adult Apprenticeship learners are funded from the employer-responsive funding model, in which all funding rates are listed as SLNs within the LSC Learning Aim Database (LAD).

Apprenticeships in the employer-responsive funding model share the same £2860 16–18 and £2775 adult national funding rates as the adult learner-responsive funding model, but there remain six key differences in the employer model:

1. Funding is paid in monthly instalments, with 25% of the NVQ and Framework funding held back for achievement.

2. Achievement funding is at framework level; for providers to claim it, all elements of the Apprenticeship have to be achieved.

3. Providers submit claims on the fourth working day of each month.

4. The fee element percentage is weighted and applied at enrolment level for all 19+ Apprenticeships.

5. Funding instalments include actual, not historical, weightings.

6. The 1.75 SLN cap per year does not apply to Apprenticeships.

The table and graph below show unweighted funding for the Level 2 Apprenticeship in Retail, as listed on the previous page.

Level 2 Retail Framework (112)	SLN	Unweighted funding	
		16–18	Adult
Total framework funding	1.505	£4304	£2401

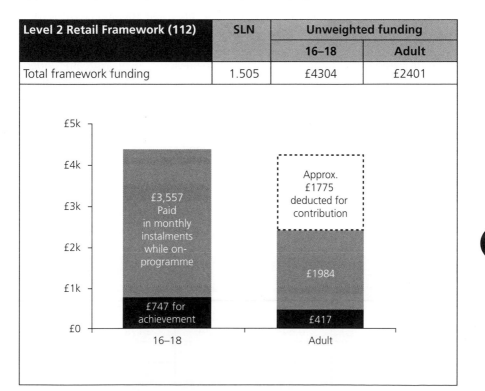

Train to Gain

In 2008/09 the LSC has brought together two types of provision within the employer-responsive model, which for the purposes of simplification is all being described as Train to Gain from 2008/09:

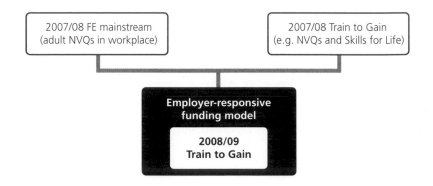

Train to Gain is 'a brokerage service which provides impartial, independent advice on training to businesses across England'. However, the term is also used to describe a rapidly expanding training scheme which was nationally rolled out in 2006 to fund full Level 2 and Skills for Life provision for adults within the workplace. In 2008/09 this has been expanded to include full Level 3 qualifications, and in most cases these qualifications are NVQs. From 2008/09 this will include NVQs delivered within the workplace that were previously FE mainstream funded. The LSC has put in place transitional arrangements to calculate the correct instalment for 'carry-in' learners from 2007/08 and number of 'flexibilities' are also being introduced to increase demand and supply (*see page 98*).

Train to Gain provision is expected to grow significantly in the next few years. Funding is planned to increase by 21% to £865m for 2008/09 and a further 45% increase to £1.3bn by 2010/11.

The national funding rate is £2775 and in June 2008 it was announced that funding rates would increase by a further 3%. This is applied as a weighting.

Programme	SLN rate		Unweighted funding	
	Higher	**Lower**	**Higher**	**Lower**
Full Level 2 (e.g. NVQ)	0.429	0.286	£1190	£794
Full Level 3 (e.g. NVQ)	0.644	0.429	£1787	£1190
Numeracy and literacy	0.18		£500	
ESOL	0.18		£500	

The higher rate funds provision that includes the initial advice, guidance and needs analysis plus support and assessment, plus a minimum of 15 hours of underpinning knowledge and understanding or substantial skills development. The lower rate is applied when the underpinning knowledge and understanding, or substantial skills development is less than 15 hours.

Note

Detailed guidance as to when the higher and lower rate should be claimed is published by the LSC, and when in doubt it is always best to ask the LSC for clarification in advance of delivering the provision.

Train to Gain is a particularly high priority for the LSC, as Skills for Life qualifications (numeracy, literacy and ESOL) and first full Level 2 and 3 learners all contribute to the government's Public Service Agreement (PSA) targets. Numeracy, literacy and all Level 2 qualifications are fully funded and as part of the new 'flexibilities' the LSC has also introduced the Level 3 entitlement in 2008/09 for those under 25 years of age. However, all other enrolments (including ESOL) are ineligible for remission, and as such they are co-funded (the fully weighted funding is reduced by the assumed contribution rate of 42.5%).

Train to Gain (unweighted)	Fully funded		Co-funded (less 42.5%)	
	Higher	**Lower**	**Higher**	**Lower**
Full Level 2	£1190	£794	N/A	N/A
Full Level 3	£1787	£1190	£1028	£685
Numeracy and literacy	£500 (plus 1.5 programme weighting)			
ESOL	£287 (plus 1.5 programme weighting)			

Train to Gain funding is paid in monthly SLN instalments, with 25% held back for when the learner achieves. The monthly instalment value is calculated as: funding divided by (months + 1). The first two instalments are paid in the first month (to reflect the higher upfront costs).

Example £1190 payment for a five-month Train to Gain enrolment:

£149 for each instalment and £298 (25%) for achievement

Dec instalment	Jan instalment	Feb instalment	Mar instalment	Apr instalment	May achievement

£0   £200   £400   £600   £800   £1000   £1200

Train to Gain – additional flexibilities

The expansion of Train to Gain has struggled to keep pace with the Government's ambitious growth plans. LSC figures published in July 2008 for 2007/08 forecast that 326,000 learners will have started, against a target of 433,750 (25% short of target). This has meant that as at the end of May the LSC has an under-spend of just over £77m and for 2008/09 the LSC targets more than double, to in excess of 600,000 Train to Gain starts.

As a result of this under-performance, combined with the requirement for significant levels of further growth, the Government has introduced 'additional flexibilities' to the programme to stimulate both demand and supply. These were signalled in June 2008 and further information was published at the end of July. However, the LSC states that 'there is still significant urgent work to be undertaken to clarify the policy, operational issues (including systems and payments) arising from these changes' and providers should visit www.lsc.gov.uk/providers/ttg/latest for updates.

Flexibilities	Description
New high funding rate threshold	The threshold for claiming the high Train to Gain funding rate has reduced from 20 to 15 hours of underpinning knowledge and understanding.
Increasing the rates by an additional 3%	As referred to on the previous page, rates are to increase over the next three years by 3% year on year (in addition to 1.5% per year inflation).
Numeracy and literacy eligible at any level	Full literacy and numeracy qualifications at Entry Level 1–3, Level 1 and Level 2 will be fully funded for learners irrespective of prior attainment. However, the expectation is that the majority of enrolments will be at Entry 3 and above (target bearing).
ESOL eligible at any level	Full ESOL qualifications at any level (including the ESOL for Work qualification) will be eligible for Train to Gain co-funding (42.5% reduction).
NVQ Level 1	Colleges delivering FE funded NVQ Level 1 qualifications in the workplace during 2007/08 can negotiate with the LSC to fund them as Train to Gain in 2008/09. These will be fully funded at the Train to Gain Level 2 higher or lower rate.
'Additional' Level 2s permitted	A limited relaxation on 'firstness' will be permitted. Up to 30% of Level 2 qualifications in any region can be 'additional' (for learners who already have the equivalent of a first full Level 2).

Flexibilities	Description
All Level 2s fully funded	All Level 2 Train to Gain qualifications will be fully funded, which is a surprise, given that 19+ Apprenticeships are co-funded and that the Level 2 Entitlement is only eligible for learners without a full Level 2.
'Additional' Level 3s	A limited relaxation on 'firstness' will be permitted for FE colleges. Up to 20% of Level 3 qualifications in any region can be for learners who already have the equivalent of a first full Level 3.
19–25 First Full Level 3 Entitlement	The 19–25 Entitlement is to be extended to Train to Gain, which means learners under 25 years of age without a first full Level 3 will be fully funded. Also, any learner of any age who does not already possess the equivalent of a first full Level 2 would be fully funded at Level 3 (Level 3 Jumpers). All other Level 3 learners would remain co-funded (42.5% reduction in funding).
Level 4/5	Colleges delivering FE funded NVQ Level 4/5 qualifications in the workplace during 2007/08 can negotiate with the LSC to fund them as Train to Gain in 2008/09. These will be co-funded (42.5% reduction) at the Train to Gain Level 3 higher or lower rate. If a learner does not already possess a full Level 2 qualification or is eligible for the 19–25 Entitlement the NVQ 4 would be fully funded.
Simplified procurement and contracting	A number of changes are being made to simplify the Train to Gain procurement and contracting process. These include awarding three-year contracts (extendable to five), making it easier for successful providers to increase the size of their contract, and moving to a single contract across all regions in 2009/10.
New range of qualifications eligible for Train to Gain	The Sector Skills Councils (SSCs) are tasked with developing Sector Qualification Strategies (SQS) which contain 'an appropriate range of fit for purpose qualifications for each sector'. Whilst 2008/09 is a transitional year, by 2009/10 only those qualifications within the SQS are likely to be funded under Train to Gain. Sector compacts will 'emerge' and the first list of SQS priority qualifications 'will be available to colleges and training providers by 1st September 2008'.

Hints and tips

The Hints and tips chapter briefly covers some other funding-related topics and additional information that may prove useful to consider.

Funding optimisation Funding optimisation is a widely used term that covers activities designed to increase funding relative to cost. At the extreme, this is a questionable practice that exploits the principles, rules and spirit of the funding guidance. However, when planning efficient and cost-effective provision there remain important things to consider. This section focuses on five of these and the LSC's *Funding Principles, Rules and Regulations*, LSC.

Target setting Targets are an increasingly important part of the funding relationship between the LSC and providers. They come in a variety of types, such as funding, SLN, learner, week, starts and success rates. They are used at different times and in different ways within different funding models, and can also be catagorised into priority and non-priority provision. This section takes a closer look at the targets and the ways to record them.

Performance monitoring Once targets have been set, the way they are monitored and reported on is important. This can lead to interventions to address performance issues before the targets have been missed. It is also important to the LSC, as it uses performance reports to alter existing contract values or as the basis for determining negotiated or tendered funding. This section also takes a closer look at the new LSC performance assessment framework, called Framework for Excellence (FfE).

Decimal-led funding The introduction of the SLN and provider factor within the new funding formula introduces the dilemma of how many decimal places to use. The number of decimal places will determine the exact amount of funding that is calculated. In reality, it may not be a significant problem, but providers need to understand that unknown decimals may be the reason they cannot match LSC funding totals. The number of decimal places is a particularly important consideration when converting SLN glh to SLN, and this chapter uses two examples to demonstrate their potential significance.

Beyond 2008/09 This guide focuses on the rules and rates of funding in 2008/09. As such, the demand-led funding formula is a significant change that will impact on many providers. However, there are a number of significant longer-term reforms that providers should be keeping a close eye on. These include: legislative reforms (raising of the compulsory education or training age to 18); curriculum reform (introduction of the Qualification and Credit Framework); structural reform (dismantling of the LSC); regulation reform (greater self-regulation for the sector); and capital reform (giving the private sector access to public funds for capital). This section takes a brief look at these in terms of what is in the pipeline for the post-16 sector.

Funding optimisation

The term funding optimisation is popular with some providers and consultants. However, the aim should always be to ensure sufficient funding is generated to deliver a high-quality service, rather than simply raising the average funding per learner (*see page 50*). There are perhaps five critical and responsible things that providers should focus on to ensure that sufficient and efficient funding is generated.

1. Check and monitor the learning aims

Learning aims determine the funding value (SLN glh), so they should be annually audited for accuracy and monitored during the year, as their rate can change.

2. Set appropriate course durations

The course duration in terms of guided learning hours (glh) will not only be important to the learner, but will also be the key determinant of cost. Therefore, given rates are described in terms of SLN glh, providers should check that their course durations (glh) do not vary wildly from LSC-listed rates (SLN glh). Also, providers should check that programme duration (a learner's total glh) does not unknowingly exceed the annual 1.75 SLN (787.5 SLN glh). Of course, providers can set durations in excess of the LSC rates, and therefore choose to cross-subsidise provision or recruit larger class sizes (*see below*).

3. Recruit and retain sufficient group sizes

It is important to remember that demand-led funding is an enrolment-based funding methodology. In other words, while the cost per group will depend on the duration, the revenue is heavily dependent on the number of enrolments. Therefore, in terms of 16–18 and adult learner-responsive funding, perhaps the most critical aspect of optimisation is class size. The funding rates are based on an expectation that there will be approximately 14 learners in a class. So, as a rule of thumb, if class sizes are smaller than 14, the course will be running at a loss. Put another way, the most efficient providers are likely to have larger classes (assuming quality does not suffer). Therefore, achieving appropriate class size targets is very important. This makes the monitoring of recruitment important, as is being able and willing to switch resources quickly, to those courses with sufficient demand.

4. Maintain high success rates

Providers with high success rates will do better than ever from the new funding formula. So, funding can be optimised by ensuring learners achieve.

5. Regularly check the validity of the data

The Individualised Learner Record (ILR) is the data that generates funding. If the ILR is incorrect, it is highly likely that the funding will also be incorrect. The LSC publishes a Data Self-Assessment Toolkit (DSAT) that providers are expected to use regularly, to check the validity of their ILR data (particularly in terms of some of the eligibility criteria).

Keep it 'in the spirit of the guidance'

The LSC has not created a funding rule for every circumstance, and therefore 'it is expected that providers will fully comply with the spirit and intention of the funding principles'. This spirit is described in the LSC's *Funding Principles, Rules and Regulations* funding guidance. In potential conflict with optimisation, it makes it clear that when planning provision, *funding should not heavily outweigh cost*.

Principles of funding learning

The funding provided to schools, colleges and other providers should reflect the directly incurred costs of efficiently delivered provision (with an appropriate contribution to overheads) within the national funding framework and rates.

All LSC providers should:

- claim funding at national rates to reflect the costs of delivery and ensure that multiple funding for provision is not claimed;

- ensure that duplication of provision in a learner's programme of study is avoided and, where this occurs because of an overlap in learning aim content, adjust the funding claimed to reflect the degree of overlap;

- consider guided learning hours (glh) as the key driver of costs incurred when determining the level of funding claimed in 16–18 and adult learner-responsive funding systems;

- consider costs of delivering provision and assessment in the workplace (together with any associated glh) as the key driver of costs incurred when determining the level of funding claimed in employer-responsive funding model;

- discuss with the LSC partnership team what funding should be claimed in circumstances where the calculation of funding to be claimed results in a level of funding that is clearly well in excess of the costs incurred;

- discuss with the LSC partnership team what funding should be claimed where providers wish to deliver provision that is in the best interests of their learners but the funding arrangement is viewed to be a barrier;

- avoid claiming LSC funding for any part of any learner's programme of study that duplicates that received from any other source, for example a different LSC funding stream, their employer or the Higher Education Funding Council for England (HEFCE).

Target-setting

Targets are clearly important, and to a great extent providers will succeed or fail according to their skill at setting and achieving appropriate targets. In fact, for a number of reasons targets have become increasingly important.

- Government funding is increasingly being targeted at those providers delivering high-quality priority provision.
- Public Service Agreement (PSA) targets have been stretched and are increasingly determining which provision receives funding.
- Reconciliation in the adult learner-responsive funding model will be based on achieving in-year and year-end priority SLN targets.
- Employer-responsive funding will only be earned once delivered.

Targets in the post-16 sector come in a variety of forms and are used at different times and in different ways within different funding models. They are also increasingly being split between priority and non-priority provision. For example, targets can be in in the form of funding, SLNs, FTEs, learner participation, starts, weeks, achievement, retention and/or success.

In the context of the LSC, many targets reside within the Summary Statement of Activity (SSoA). The SSoA was introduced by the LSC in 2007/08, and is a numerical summary of provision the LSC is funding. It contains a complex and detailed range of funding, learner participation and SLN figures for three funding models, along with such other targets as full-cost income. Providers negotiate targets within the SSoA with the LSC, and the LSC then inputs the targets via an online tool called the Planning and Modelling System (PaMS). Providers can log into PaMS to view their targets and their previous years' performance.

Note

The SSoA is a national template with national counting methodologies, both of which are available online. However, some regional LSCs have adopted either different or additional approaches to targets and the SSoA. It is therefore advisable for providers to consider both the national and the regional arrangements when it comes to target-setting and monitoring performance.

Hints and tips for target-setting

- Always be clear about the difference between an enrolment and a learner target. This is particularly important where a learner is enrolled on two PSA target-bearing qualifications (such as literacy and an NVQ 2). In this case, the learner target is one, yet the PSA sub-targets added together equal two. Therefore, at qualification level in a template such as the SSoA, there should be an expectation that the priority sub-targets will often exceed the total learner target.

- Always use the Learning Aim Database (LAD) to determine which qualifications do and do not contribute to PSA targets.
- Participation targets include all learners who are on-programme during the given year. This means that learners who have a start and end date in more than one academic year become 'carry-in' learners for the second year. These learners are effectively counted twice, as they count towards the participation target in the first year, and will count towards the participation target in the following year. Providers need to be aware of carry-in learners as they will generate only a proportion of the total funding in the year in question. In terms of a sales (new business) targets it is therefore advisable to separate carry-in from new starts (particularly within the employer-responsive funding model).
- Many providers plan at learner group level with target class sizes. The splitting of FE mainstream into different funding models makes the setting of sub-targets for mixed cohorts all the more important.

A college may set targets and calculate funding as follows:

Madeup College group (see page 40)	Target	of which (sub-targets)		
		16–18 remitted	19+ fully funded	19 co-funded
Learners in the group	18	10	6	2
SLN per learner	1.2	1.2	1.2	1.2
Total SLN	21.6	12	7.2	2.4
Funding rate	n/a	£2860	£2775	£1981
Provider factor	n/a	1.333	1.486	1.486
LSC funding total	£82,505	£45,749	£29,690	£7066

This group is therefore contributing £45,749 towards the 16–18 model allocation and £36,756 towards the adult learner-responsive allocation.

Setting sub-targets in this way also means that the provider factor can be altered at course level (such as by incorporating the actual programme weighting rather than the average) to help set more reliable departmental or cost centre funding targets.

- It is important to remember that the definition of a start has changed in 2008/09 (see page 48). In terms of full-time learners, this is likely to mean that if a provider does not alter delivery, fewer learners will count towards learner targets in 2008/09. This is because learners starting in mid-September will have to stay on-programme for six weeks (four weeks more than in 2007/08). The impact of this change should be considered when setting targets and comparing 2007/08 and 2008/09 performance.

Performance monitoring

Once provision has been planned and funding targets have been set, it is then important to monitor performance during the year. To do this, it is worth considering two areas of the demand-led funding formula for the 16–18 and adult learner-responsive funding models:

1. Once the enrolment has passed the minimum period (*see page 48*), all of the funding is guaranteed in the given academic year. This is far simpler than the previous further education methodology, which had tri-annual census dates and the timing of the withdrawal relative to the last census date reduced the funding claim. This change should make year-end forecasts during the year far easier.

2. The use of a fixed provider factor for all provision may make it unreliable to compare relative expenditure and funding at departmental level. Primarily this is because an average programme weighting has been used. Although it may not be a perfect solution, try applying course level provider factors to set funding targets.

The LSC will give particular attention to employer-responsive provision, and adjust contract values where necessary (probably on a quarterly basis). However, it also uses a range of performance reports, some of which are within the Online Planning and Modelling System (PaMS) (*see page 104*).

Minimum Levels of Performance (MLP) reports were introduced in 2006 and contain weighted success rates with various performance thresholds for provision by duration, level and sector. If insufficient provision is above the threshold, a provider is served with a formal notice to improve (NTI). If, the following year, the provision remains below the threshold, the LSC could choose to stop funding the poorly performing provision. This might result in the LSC seeking an alternative provider via open competitive tendering.

MLPs are the forerunner of a more comprehensive performance framework being introduced in 2008/09, known as the Framework for Excellence (FfE). The Framework is far wider and more complex than MLPs, as it includes more than 15 grades within the areas of responsiveness, effectiveness and finance. The Framework will be used for colleges and training providers in 2008/09, and school sixth forms may be included from 2009/10.

The Framework scores (outstanding, good, satisfactory or unsatisfactory) will be published and used to inform learners and employers, and the funding bodies' commissioning decisions. Performance in 2008/09 will determine the first full round of published FfE grades. This means they will be published in the spring of 2010 so that they can be used just in time to inform the tendering round for 2010/11. The FfE is entering a second phase of pilots in the summer of 2008, although the current design is summarised on page 107. More detailed information, which is updated as the FfE evolves, can be accessed from the LSC website (http://ffe.lsc.gov.uk/).

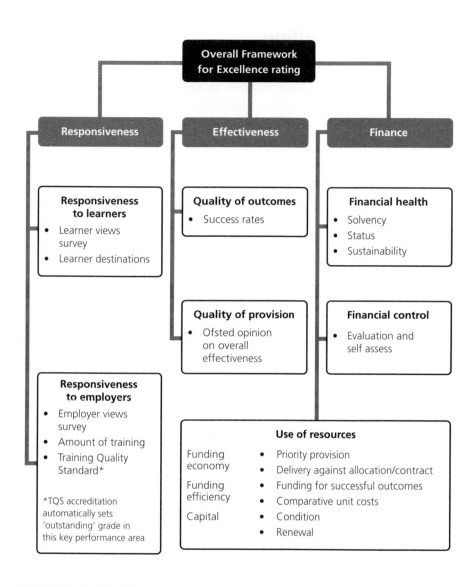

Overall Framework for Excellence rating

Responsiveness

Effectiveness

Finance

Responsiveness to learners
- Learner views survey
- Learner destinations

Responsiveness to employers
- Employer views survey
- Amount of training
- Training Quality Standard*

*TQS accreditation automatically sets 'outstanding' grade in this key performance area

Quality of outcomes
- Success rates

Quality of provision
- Ofsted opinion on overall effectiveness

Use of resources

Funding economy	• Priority provision
	• Delivery against allocation/contract
Funding efficiency	• Funding for successful outcomes
	• Comparative unit costs
Capital	• Condition
	• Renewal

Financial health
- Solvency
- Status
- Sustainability

Financial control
- Evaluation and self assess

The Framework should be used by colleges and providers to assess and improve their own performance, and incorporated into reporting mechanisms to governors and sponsors. In addition, the LSC will expect providers to use the performance ratings as part of the evidence for self-assessment from the academic year 2008/09. The revised inspection handbook for September 2008 will include information on how inspectors will begin to use performance scores from the Framework. The Framework will be incorporated into the LSC's business cycle and processes for commissioning, procurement, challenging performance and intervention, including financial intervention, by 2010.

Source: *LSC Grant Letter 2008–09*, DIUS (November 2007)

Decimal-led funding

The demand-led national funding formula is significantly different from that which came before, not least because Standard Learner Numbers (SLNs) come with decimal places. In the 16–18 and adult learner-responsive model the LSC does not actually publish the SLNs, it publishes the SLN in terms of guided learning hours (SLN glh). The SLN glh is then converted into an SLN by dividing it by 450 (*see page 32*).

For example, an AS-level qualification taught during the day has a listed rate of 150 SLN glh, which is then divided by 450 to determine the SLN rate. Is this SLN rate 0.3, 0.33, 0.333 or 0.3333? All these answers are of course correct, as an AS-level is worth one third of one SLN, which is 0.3 SLN recurring. The number of decimal paces used for the SLN will impact on the total funding. For example, with a £2860 funding rate, 0.3 SLN generates £858 while 0.3333 SLN generates £953.

SLN decimal places can make a significant difference, as shown below.

Example of unweighted funding for AS-level qualifications

150 SLN glh	1 decimal	2 decimal	3 decimal	4 decimal
SLN glh / 450	0.3	0.33	0.333	0.3333
Learners	2000	2000	2000	2000
AS per learner	4	4	4	4
Total SLN	2400	2640	2664	2666
Funding rate	£2860	£2860	£2860	£2860
Funding	£6,864,000	£7,550,400	£7,619,040	£7,625,904
Increase beyond 1 decimal		£686,400	£755,040	£761,904

There are many qualifications where this presents a problem, one of which is the full time NVQ. This is listed at 520 SLN glh. Once divided by 450, this is 1.1555555555555555555555555555555555555555r SLN.

In the example shown in the graph below, every additional decimal place for a full-time NVQ SLN reduces funding.

Example of unweighted funding for full-time NVQ qualifications

520 SLN glh	1 decimal	2 decimal	3 decimal	4 decimal
SLN glh / 450	1.2	1.16	1.156	1.1556
Learners	2000	2000	2000	2000
NVQ per learner	1	1	1	1
Total SLN	2400	2320	2312	2311
Funding rate	£2860	£2860	£2860	£2860
Funding	£6,864,000	£6,635,200	£6,612,320	£6,610,032
Decrease beyond 1 decimal		−£228,800	−£251,680	−£253,968

The same problem occurs with the elements within, and calculation for, the provider factor (see page 36). These are published for each provider by the LSC, rounded to three decimal places, but in reality they will run to many more.

To be fair, beyond three decimal places the impact is small and the LSC software will use many more, but this does raise two important points:
1. When planning provision, use at least three decimal places for SLNs.
2. Decimal places may be the reason you cannot agree the total in an LSC funding calculation. You may get close, but it is unlikely the pounds and/or pence will be the same, unless the full SLN and provider factor (with decimal places) match in both calculations.

Beyond 2008/09

The funding formula changes represent a small part of a wider package of reforms that are worthy of a mention here. This section summarises a number of reforms that providers should keep an eye on, as in the coming years they will have a significant impact on the way post-16 funding is to be distributed.

Curriculum reform

The introduction of the diplomas in 2008/09 represents the start of very significant qualification strategies and reforms to the curriculum structures.

- In March 2008 the Department for Children, Schools and Families (DCSF) launched the consultation *Promoting achievement, valuing success: a strategy for 14–19 qualifications*. The paper describes the setting up of a new framework for determining which qualifications can be funded until 2012, the creation of a Joint Advisory Committee for Qualifications Approval (JACQA) and the commitment to 'move to a single credit-based framework for 14–19 qualifications by 2013'.

- In 2006 the tests and trials of the new Qualification and Credit Framework (QCF) began. The QCF will be phased in from 2008/09 and will gradually replace the National Qualifications Framework (NQF). The intention is that only those qualifications on the QCF will be eligible for funding. Also, the UK Vocational Qualification Reform Programme (UKVQRP) is being led by the Sector Skills Councils to make qualifications QCF-compatible. This will enable the LSC to 'align public funding to priority qualifications' for 2009/10.

Legislative reform

A number of the changes that will impact on the distribution of post-16 funding and eligibility require legislation.

- The *Further Education and Training Act 2007* provides 'FE institutions in England the power to award foundation degrees'.

- The *Education and Skills Bill of 2007–08* introduced the provision for raising the compulsory age of participation in education or training to 17-year-olds by 2013 and 18-year-olds by 2015.

- The consultation document *Time to Train*, DIUS (June 2008) includes a new legal right to request time to train, as well as a statutory entitlement to an Apprenticeship place for all eligible young people. The consultation also provides the platform to implement structural reform to include the transfer of 16–19 funding from the LSC to local authorities.

Structural reform

In March 2008 the Department for Children, Schools and Families (DCSF) and the Department for Innovation, Universities and Schools (DIUS) jointly launched a consultation called *Raising Expectations: enabling the system to deliver*, DCSF, DIUS (March 2008). Also referred to as the Machinery of Government consultation, it contains detailed plans to replace the LSC with a number of new national funding bodies, as well as to transfer the 16–19 funding to local authorities.

Planned machinery of government from 2010

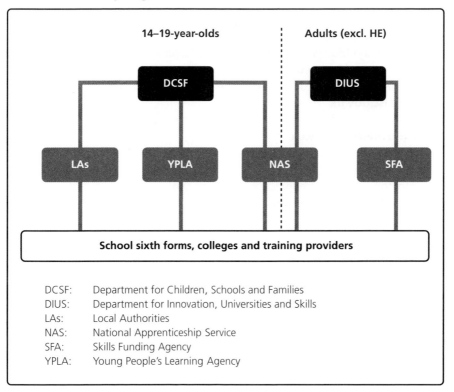

DCSF:	Department for Children, Schools and Families
DIUS:	Department for Innovation, Universities and Skills
LAs:	Local Authorities
NAS:	National Apprenticeship Service
SFA:	Skills Funding Agency
YPLA:	Young People's Learning Agency

Regulatory reform

In 2006 the Government issued a challenge to the further education sector to take collective responsibility for its own future destiny and reputation and thus forge a new relationship with Government. This led to the establishment of the Self Regulation Implementation Group, and in June 2008 a new sector owned organisation called the Learning and Skills Improvement Service (LSIS) was launched.

Capital reform

Schools and colleges are benefiting from capital projects funded by the LSC. The LSC will extend this funding to private-sector training providers.

Web resources

The following is a list of useful websites that contain information about post-16 funding, data and qualifications. To download documents referred to in this guide, visit the official website at **www.fundingguide.co.uk**

LSC websites
www.lsc.gov.uk
The Learning and Skills Council homepage
http://research.lsc.gov.uk
The homepage for LSC research
http://pam.lsc.gov.uk
The Planning and Modelling System (PaMS) homepage (*see page 104*)
https://gateway.lsc.gov.uk
Provider Gateway, for document exchange and access to PaMS
http://ffe.lsc.gov.uk
The LSC Framework for Excellence homepage (*see page 107*)
http://providers.lsc.gov.uk
Provider extranet for Online Data Collection Portal and LAD
http://e2e.lsc.gov.uk
The Entry to Employment homepage (*see page 90*)
https://lsc.bravosolution.com
The Learning and Skills eTendering Portal

Qualification websites
www.edexcel.org.uk/quals
Edexcel's suite of qualifications
www.qca.org.uk
The Qualifications and Curriculum Authority
www.ofqual.gov.uk
The Office of the Qualifications and Examinations Regulator
www.accreditedqualifications.org.uk
The National Database of Accredited Qualifications
www.Apprenticeships.org.uk
The Apprenticeship website, containing all the frameworks (*see page 94*)
http://www.dfes.gov.uk/section96
The Government website for qualifications for those under 19 years old
http://www.dfes.gov.uk/section97
The Government website for qualifications for those over 18 years old
http://yp.direct.gov.uk/diplomas
The Government website for the new 14–19 diploma (*see page 80*)
http://qfr.lsc.gov.uk
The LSC's Qualification and Framework Reform homepage
http://providers.lsc.gov.uk/LAD
The LSC's Learning Aim Database (downloads and search engine)

Government websites

www.dius.gov.uk
The Department for Innovation, Universities and Skills
www.dcsf.gov.uk
The Department for Children, Schools and Families
www.dwp.gov.uk
The Department for Work and Pensions
www.traintogain.gov.uk
The official Train to Gain website (*see page 96*)

Data websites

www.theia.org.uk
The Information Authority, who publish the ILR specification
www.miap.gov.uk
Managing Information Across Partners, who handle the sharing of data
www.lsc.gov.uk/providers/data
The area on the LSC website for data, news and software downloads
www.jisc.ac.uk
The Joint Information Systems Committee homepage

Other agencies

www.ukces.org.uk
The UK Commission for Employment and Skills
www.sscalliance.org
The Alliance of Sector Skills Councils
www.ofsted.gov.uk
The Office for Standards in Education

Selection of websites with useful and free recourses

www.fundingguide.co.uk
The official homepage for this practical guide to funding
www.edexcel.org.uk/about/policies/funding
Sign up to receive or download Edexcel's Funding Watch papers
www.edexcel.org.uk/about/policies/epw
Sign up to receive or download Edexcel's Policy Watch papers
www.lewisham.ac.uk/pf
Lewisham College's homepage for funding, training and free resources
www.aoc.co.uk
The Association of Colleges
www.learningproviders.org.uk
The Association of Learning Providers
www.lsneducation.org.uk
The Learning and Skills Network
www.niace.org.uk
The National Institute of Adult Continuing Education

Notes

If you are a provider, you can use this section to fill in your own figures.

Provider factor elements	16–18	Adult learner
Programme weighting		
Disadvantage uplift		
Area costs uplift		
Short programme modifier		
Success factor		

Provider factor (PF)

Provider factor elements	16–18 Apprenticeship	Employer model
Programme weighting		
Disadvantage uplift		
Area costs uplift		
Short programme modifier		
Retention and achievement factor		

Provider factor (PF)

Funding rates (national or transitional)	Funding rate (FR)
16–18 (excl. Apprenticeships)	
16–18 Apprenticeships	
Employer-responsive	
Employer--responsive co-funded rate	
Adult learner-responsive	
Adult learner-responsive co-funded rate	

16–18 Model	SLN	x	FR	x	PF	+	ALS
Fully funded learners							

2008/09 Allocation

16–18 Apprenticeship	SLN	x	FR	x	PF	+	ALS
Fully funded learners							

2008/09 Allocation

Employer-responsive	SLN	x	FR	x	PF	+	ALS
Fully funded learners							
Co-funded learners							

2008/09 Allocation

Adult learner-responsive	SLN	x	FR	x	PF	+	ALS
Fully funded learners							
Co-funded learners							

2008/09 Allocation

Total formula funding	Total 2008/09 allocation
16–18 (excl. Apprenticeships)	
16–18 Apprenticeships	
Employer-responsive	
Adult learner-responsive	

Total 2008/09 allocation